POEMS
OF
Faith

Inspiring Verse for
Strength and Comfort

EDITED BY BOB BLAISDELL

ixia
PRESS

Garden City, New York

To Ramona Carbotte
—B.B.

Copyright

Bibliographical Note

This Ixia Press edition, first published in 2022, is an unabridged republication of the work first published by Dover Publications in 2002.

Library of Congress Cataloging-in-Publication Data

Names: Blaisdell, Robert, editor.
Title: Poems of faith : inspiring verse for strength and comfort / edited by Bob Blaisdell.
Description: Garden City, New York : Ixia Press, 2022. | Includes index. | Summary: "Poetry has long been a source of comfort and inspiration in times of struggle and celebration, and this carefully curated selection of nearly 100 American and British poems offers readers a profound collection of verse for those who are steadfast in their faith or those who are looking to renew it. This beautiful gift edition includes two of John Donne's "Holy Sonnets," Ben Jonson's "To the Holy Trinity," Christina Rosetti's "Wrestling," and Emily Brontë's "Last Lines" as well as poems by Andrew Marvell, Gerard Manley Hopkins, William Blake, Emily Dickinson, and Elizabeth Barrett Browning"—Provided by publisher.
Identifiers: LCCN 2021021971 | ISBN 9780486849232 (hardcover)
Subjects: LCSH: Religious poetry, American. | Religious poetry, English. | Inspiration—Poetry. | Conduct of life—Poetry. | LCGFT: Religious poetry.
Classification: LCC PS595.R4 P58 2022 | DDC 811.008/0382—dc23
LC record available at https://lccn.loc.gov/2021021971

Ixia Press
An imprint of Dover Publications

Manufactured in the United States of America
84923601   2021
www.doverpublications.com/ixiapress

Note

Most of these hundred poems from five hundred years of English verse relate the success of the individual "sinner" in overcoming his faint heart and rediscovering, strengthening, or retuning his faith. "How should I praise thee, Lord! how should my rhymes/Gladly engrave thy love in steel,/If what my soul doth feel sometimes,/My soul might ever feel!" writes the supreme poet on Christian faith, George Herbert, in "The Temper." Herbert and all the various, individual, and distinct voices in this collection dramatize how we use our minds and hearts to pursue faith, to clutch it, and yet—as with its complementary feelings of joy and peace—we inevitably lose our grasp of it. Achieved, inside us, it seems to have come from without, given by grace rather than our virtue; lost, outside us, it seems maddeningly unattainable. The story gets told over and over, down the centuries; there is a crisis of faith, there is doubt or fear or despair, and faith is restored, by what seems a gift of grace, or by a glimpse of the larger context of our experience. The poetry of faith, no matter what its religious origin, is an effort to experience a simple and yet surprisingly difficult truth: "Being is good."

As much as we delight in the dramas of crisis and recovery, we can marvel, also, at their authors' variety of experiences and temperaments. We must admire the candor with which they examine their loss of purpose and trust. They are telling us what it is to be human; the striving for faith is a continuous effort of imagination, the effort to make contact with what is outside ourselves and to feel a part of it. The eighteenth-century English poet William Cowper reflects in "Peace after a Storm":

When darkness long has veiled my mind,
  And smiling day once more appears,
Then, my Redeemer, then I find
  The folly of my doubts and fears.

Straight I upbraid my wandering heart,
  And blush that I should ever be
Thus prone to act so base a part,
  Or harbor one hard thought of thee.

Oh! let me then at length be taught
  What I am still so slow to learn;
That God is Love, and changes not,
  Nor knows the shadow of a turn.

Sweet truth, and easy to repeat!
  But when my faith is sharply tried,
I find myself a learner yet,
  Unskilful, weak, and apt to slide.

Some writers are wrestling with doubt of their own beliefs. Others find themselves having strayed from the essentials as a consequence of the indiscipline of their own minds. In "Confusion," Christopher Harvey is "unraveling":

O! How my mind
      Is gravel'd!*
              Not a thought
That I can find
      But's ravel'd
              All to nought.

---

* *gravel'd]* perplexed

Short ends of threads,
    And narrow shreds,
        Of lists,
Knots snarled ruffs,
    Loose broken tufts
        Of twists,
Are my torn meditation's ragged clothing,

There is also the doubt that comes from suffering, from the world itself, as in "The Doubter's Prayer," where Anne Brontë beseeches the Lord:

Oh, help me, God! For Thou alone
    Canst my distracted soul relieve;
Forsake it not, it is Thine own,
    Though weak, yet longing to believe.

Oh, drive these cruel doubts away;
    And make me know that Thou art God!
A faith, that shines by night and day,
    Will lighten every earthly load.

Then there is the idea of faith as a necessary component of understanding; the philosopher George Santayana suggests in a sonnet that we "Bid, then, the tender light of faith to shine/By which alone the mortal heart is led/Unto the thinking of the thought divine." Faith can be a source of intellectual humility and honesty: "Though reason cannot through faith's myst'ries see,/It sees that there and such they be," writes Abraham Cowley, a contemporary of the metaphysical poet Henry Vaughan. The poets may resign themselves to not knowing the nature of God, but they rarely suppress their curiosity and wonder to know it. Thomas Traherne, in "Insatiableness," exclaims:

> No Walls confine! Can nothing hold my Mind!
> Can I no Rest nor Satisfaction find?
>   Must I behold Eternity
>   And see
>   What Things above the Heav'ns be?

Traherne shows us that wonder, a sense of the immanently marvelous, is one of the gifts that comes with faith, along with redemption from suffering, doubt, and the sense of our own unworthiness. It seems necessary to our feeling of well-being to believe that God or the Universe loves us and includes us in its purposes. We need this trust, but it is difficult to sustain. Challenges to faith come all the time, from the natural disasters of human life—loss of jobs, health, loved ones, money. Or without those, our own inner self-doubts—our desires and vanities, our griefs and smaller miseries—bedevil us. We keep having to start over again to find some kind of reconciliation and peace, get our priorities in order, and maintain inner decorum and openness of heart.

> These are thy wonders, Lord of love!
> To make us see we are but flow'rs that glide:
> Which when we once can find and prove,
> Thou hast a garden for us, where to 'bide.
> Who would be more,
> Swelling through store,
> Forfeit their Paradise by their pride.
>   —George Herbert, "The Flower"

Among the poets of faith, shoulder to shoulder with George Herbert, Christina Georgina Rossetti, and Gerard Manley Hopkins, we find relatively obscure but fabulously ecstatic poets such as Christopher Harvey, whose "Sacred Poems and Private Ejaculations" were written "in imitation of" Herbert; John Newton, the reformed slave-trader who became a popular composer of hymns; James Clarence Mangan, the troubled Irish songwriter and translator; and Digby Mackworth Dolben, a friend and contemporary of Robert Bridges who died at nineteen. These poets' heartfelt, passionate outpourings of love and dependence still speak to us across countries and centuries. Many conclude on a note of gratitude, the natural next thought:

> Without thy presence, wealth is bags of cares;
> Wisdom, but folly; joy, disquiet—sadness:
> Friendship is treason, and delights are snares;
> Pleasures but pain, and mirth but pleasing madness:
> Without thee, Lord, things be not what they be,
> Nor have they being, when compar'd with thee.
> —Francis Quarles, "Delight in God Only"

—Bob Blaisdell and Kia Penso

*

My professional gratitude goes to the editors and compilers of earlier collections of Christian poetry in English; they have brought to my attention a wonderful variety of authors. Particularly helpful have been Reverend Richard Cattermole's *Sacred Poetry of the Seventeenth Century* (1835), Lord David Cecil's *The Oxford Book of Christian Verse* (1940), and Robert Atwan and Laurance Wieder's *Chapters into Verse: Poetry in English Inspired by The Bible* (1993).

I am grateful also to my friends and colleagues who suggested particular authors and works: Robyn Bell, Lea Fridman, Daniel Kane, Kia Penso, and John Wilson. For helping me obtain obscure texts, I thank the microfilm and rare book librarians of Columbia University's Butler Library and the research librarians at the New York Public Library.

—B.B.

Contents

Ben Jonson (1574–1637)

George Sandys (1577–1643)

George Wither (1588–1667)

Henry King (1591–1669)

Robert Herrick (1591–1674)

Francis Quarles (1592–1664)

George Herbert (1593–1632)

Anonymous (c. 1539)

To the Book

Go, little Book, get thee acquaintance
  Among the lovers of God's word,
Give them occasion the same to a'vance,
  And to make their songs of the Lord,
That they may thrust under the board
  All other Ballads of filthiness,
And that we all with one accord
  May give ensample of godliness.

Go, little Book, among men's children,
  And get thee to their company;
Teach them to sing the Commandments Ten,
  And other Ballads of God's glory:
Be not ashamed, I warrant thee,
  Though thou be rude in song and rhyme,
Thou shalt to youth some occasion be,
  In godly sports to pass their time.

The Lamentation of a Sinner

O Lord, in Thee is all my trust,
  give ear unto my woeful cry:
Refuse me not that am unjust,
  but bowing down Thy heavenly eye,
Behold how I do still lament
  my sins wherein I do offend;
O Lord, for them shall I be shunned,
  when Thee to please I do intend?

No, no, not so Thy will is bent,
    to deal with sinners in Thine ire;
But when in heart they shall repent,
    Thou grantst with speed their just desire:
To Thee therefore still shall I cry
    to wash away my sinful crime:
Thy blood (O Lord) is not yet dry
    but that Thou may help me in time.

For why will I on earth remain
    oppressed, alas!, with woe and grief?
My feeble heart plunged in pain,
    doth sigh and sough for Thy relief.
Sweet Christ, will Thou not then appear,
    to comfort them that comfort lack?
Will Thou not bow Thine ear to hear?
    Lord Jesus, come and be not slack!

For then shall Thine receive their rest;
    their joy, their bliss, their perfect peace,
And see Thy face of treasure best,
    O Lord, that does our joys increase.
Then shall Thou give those Noble crowns,
    which Thine own blood has dearly bought.
Then shall those Psalms and high Renowns
    be given in grace most richly wrought.

Then shall Thy Saints redeemed dear,
    from bail to bliss removed be:

And sweet Christ, Thy sweet voice hear
  come unto me babes, come to me.
Come Reign in joy Eternally,
  come reign in bliss that has no end,
Come therefore, Lord! Come, Christ, we pray,
  our pressed grief with speed amend.

Haste Thee, O Lord, haste thee, I say,
  to pour on me the gifts of grace;
That when this life must flit away,
  in heaven with Thee I may have place.
Where Thou dost reign eternally,
  with God, which once did down thee send,
Where Angels sing continually,
  to Thee be praise, world without end.

So be it.

∾

Anonymous (c. 1558)

"God be in my head"

God be in my head,
And in my understanding;

God be in mine eyes,
And in my looking;

God be in my mouth,
And in my speaking;

God be in my heart,
And in my thinking;

God be at mine end,
And at my departing.

✍

George Gascoigne (1525?–1577)

De Profundis

From depth of dole wherein my soul doth dwell,
From heavy heart which harbours in my breast,
From troubled sprite which seldom taketh rest,
From hope of heaven, from dread of darksome hell,
O gracious God, to thee I cry and yell:
My God, my Lord, my lovely Lord alone,
To thee I call, to thee I make my moan.
And thou, good God, vouchsafe in grace to take
    This woful plaint
    Wherein I faint:—
Oh, hear me then, for thy great mercy's sake!

Oh, bend thine ears attentively to hear;
Oh, turn thine eyes—behold me now I wail;
Oh, hearken, Lord, give ear for mine avail;
Oh, mark in mind the burdens that I bear!
See how I sink in sorrows everywhere;

Behold and see what dolours I endure;
Give ear and mark what plaints I put in ure;
Bend willing ears, and pity therewithal
      My wailing voice,
      Which hath no choice
But evermore upon thy name to call.

If thou, good Lord, shouldst take thy rod in hand,
If thou regard what sins are daily done,
If thou take hold where we our works begun,
If thou decree in judgment for to stand
And be extreme to see our 'scuses scann'd,—
If thou take note of every thing amiss,
And write in rolls how frail our nature is,
O glorious God! O King! O Prince of power!
      What mortal wight
      May then have light
To feel thy frown, if thou have list to lower?

But thou art good, and hast of mercy store;
Thou not delight'st to see a sinner fall;
Thou hearkenest first before we come to call;
Thy ears are set wide open evermore;
Before we knock thou comest to the door;
Thou art more prest to hear a sinner cry,
Than he is quick to climb to thee on high.
Thy mighty name be praised then alway:
      Let faith and fear
      True witness bear,

How fast they stand which on thy mercy stay.
I look for thee, my lovely Lord, therefore;
For thee I wait, for thee I tarry still;
Mine eyes do long to gaze on thee my fill;
For thee I watch, for thee I pry and pore;
My soul for thee attendeth evermore;
My soul doth thirst to take of thee a taste;
My soul desires with thee for to be placed;
And to thy word, which can no man deceive,—
  Mine only trust,
  My love and lust,—
In confidence continually shall cleave.

Before the break or dawning of the day,
Before the light be seen in lofty skies,
Before the sun appear in pleasant wise,
Before the watch—before the watch, I say,
Before the ward that waits therefore alway,
My soul, my sense, my secret thought, my sprite,
My will, my wish, my joy, and my delight,
Unto the Lord, that sits in heaven on high,
  With hasty wing,
  From me doth fling,
And striveth still unto the Lord to fly.

O Israel, O household of the Lord,
O Abraham's sons, O brood of blessed seed—
O chosen sheep, that fear the Lord indeed—
O hungry hearts, feed still upon his word,
And put your trust in him with one accord!

For he hath mercy evermore at hand;
His fountains flow, his springs do never stand;
And plenteously he loveth to redeem
  Such sinners all
  As on him call,
And faithfully his mercies most esteem.

He will redeem our deadly, drooping state;
He will bring home the sheep that go astray;
He will help them that hope in him alway;
He will appease our discord and debate,
He will soon save, though we repent us late.
He will be ours if we continue his;
He will bring bale to joy and perfect bliss;
He will redeem the flock of his elect
  From all that is,
  Or was, amiss,
Since Abraham's heirs did first his laws reject.

Sir Philip Sidney (1554–1586)

"Leave me, O Love, which reachest but to dust"

Leave me, O Love, which reachest but to dust;
And thou, my mind, aspire to higher things;
Grow rich in that which never taketh rust;
Whatever fades, but fading pleasure brings.

Draw in thy beams, and humble all thy might
To that sweet yoke where lasting freedoms be,
Which breaks the clouds, and opens forth the light,
That doth both shine and give us sight to see.
Oh, take fast hold; let that light be thy guide
In this small course which birth draws out to death,
And think how evil becometh him to slide,
Who seeketh heaven, and comes of heavenly breath.
  Then farewell, world; thy uttermost I see:
  Eternal Love, maintain thy life in me.

ᕦᕤ

Robert Southwell (1560–1595)

A Preparative to Prayer

When thou dost talk with God—by prayer, I mean—
Lift up pure hands, lay down all lust's desires;
Fix thoughts on heaven, present a conscience clean:
Such holy blame to mercy's throne aspires.
Confess fault's guilt, crave pardon for thy sin,
Tread holy paths, call grace to guide therein.

It is the spirit with reverence must obey
Our Maker's will, to practise what he taught:
Make not the flesh thy counsel when thou pray;
'Tis enemy to every virtuous thought;
It is the foe we daily feed and clothe;
It is the prison that the soul doth loathe.

Even as Elias, mounting to the sky,
Did cast his mantle to the earth behind;
So when the heart presents the prayer on high,
Exclude the world from traffic with the mind:
Lips near to God, and ranging heart within,
Is but vain babbling, and converts to sin.

Like Abraham ascending up the hill
To sacrifice, his servants left below,
That he might act the great commander's will,
Without impeach to his obedient blow;
Even so the soul, remote from earthly things,
Should mount salvation's shelter—mercy's wings.

Mary Sidney, Countess of Pembroke (1561–1621)

Psalm 139

Domine, probasti

O Lord in me there lieth nought,
But to thy search revealèd lies:
For when I sit
Thou markest it:
No less thou notest when I rise:
Yea closest closet of my thought
Hath open windows to thine eyes.

Thou walkest with me when I walk,
　　When to my bed for rest I go,
　　　　I find thee there,
　　　　And ev'ry where:
　　Not youngest thought in me doth grow,
No, not one word I cast to talk,
　　But yet unutt'red thou dost know.

If forth I march, thou goest before,
　　If back I turn, thou com'st behind:
　　　　So forth nor back
　　　　Thy guard I lack,
　　Nay on me too thy hand I find.
Well I thy wisdom may adore,
　　But never reach with earthy mind.

To shun thy notice, leave thine eye,
　　O whither might I take my way?
　　　　To starry sphere?
　　　　Thy throne is there.
　　To dead men's undelightsome stay?
There is thy walk, and there to lie
　　Unknown, in vain I should assay.

O Sun, whom light nor flight can match,
　　Suppose thy lightful, flightful wings
　　　　Thou lend to me
　　　　And I could flee
　　As far as thee the ev'ning brings:
Ev'n led to West he would me catch,
　　Nor should I lurk with western things.

Do thou thy best, O secret night,
In sable vail to cover me:
Thy sable vail
Shall vainly fail:
With day unmask'd my night shall be,
For night is day, and darkness light,
O father of all lights to thee.

Each inmost peace in me is thine,
While yet I in my mother dwelt,
All that me clad
From thee I had.
Thou in my frame hast strangely dealt:
Needs in my praise thy works must shine,
So inly them my thoughts have felt.

Thou, how my back was beam-wise laid,
And raftring of my ribs dost know:
Know'st ev'ry point
Of bone and joint,
How to this whole these parts did grow,
In brave embroid'ry fair arrayed,
Though wrought in shop both dark and low.

Nay, fashionless, ere form I took,
Thy all and more beholding eye
My shapeless shape
Could not escape:
All these times fram'd successively,

Ere one had being, in the book
    Of thy foresight enrol'd did lie.

My God, how I these studies prize,
    That do thy hidden workings show!
        Whose sum is such,
        No sum so much:
    Nay sum'd as sand they endless grow.
I lie to sleep, from sleep I rise,
    Yet still in thought with thee I go.

My God, if thou but one wouldst kill,
    Then straight would leave my further chase,
        This cursed brood
        Inur'd to blood:
    Whose graceless taunts at thy disgrace
Have aimed oft: and hating still
    Would with proud lies thy truth outface.

Hate not I them who thee do hate?
    Thine, Lord, I will the censure be.
        Detest I not
        The cankered knot
    Whom I against thee banded see?
O Lord, thou know'st in highest rate
    I hate them all as foes to me.

Search me, my God, and prove my heart,
    Examine me, and try my thought,

> And mark in me
> If ought there be
> That hath with cause their anger wrought.
> If not (as not) my lives each part,
> Lord, safely guide from danger brought.

Michael Drayton (1563–1631)

The Song of Jonah in the Whale's Belly

In grief and anguish of my heart, my voice I did extend
Unto the Lord, and he thereto a willing care did lend;
Even from the deep and darkest pit and the infernal lake,
To me he hath bow'd down his ear, for his great mercy's sake.
For thou into the midst of surging seas so deep
Hast cast me forth, whose bottom is so low and wondrous
    steep;
Whose mighty wallowing waves, which from the floods do
    flow,
Have with their power up swallowed me, and overwhelm'd
    me though.
Then said I, lo! I am exil'd from presence of thy face!
Yet will I once again behold thy house and dwelling place:
The waters have encompast me, the floods inclosed me
    round,
The weeds have sore encumbered me, which in the seas
    abound:

Unto the valleys down I went, beneath the hills which stand;
The earth hath there environ'd me with force of all the land:
Yet hast thou still preserved me from all these dangers here,
And brought my life out of the pit, oh Lord, my God so
    dear!
My soul consuming thus with care, I prayed unto the Lord,
And he from out his holy place heard me with one accord.
Who to vain lying vanities doth wholly him betake
Doth err, also God's mercy he doth utterly forsake:
But I will offer unto him the sacrifice of praise,
And pay my vows, ascribing thanks unto the Lord always.

A Song of the Faithful

Lord, at thy voice my heart for fear hath trembled:
Unto the world, Lord, let thy works be showen;
In these our days now let thy power be knowen,
And yet in wrath let mercy be remembred.

From Teman, lo! our God you may behold,
The Holy One from Paran mount so high!
His glory hath clean covered the sky,
And in the earth his praises be enrolled.

His shining was more clearer than the light;
And from his hands a fullness did proceed,
Which did contain his wrath and power indeed;
Consuming plagues and fire were in his sight.

He stood aloft and compassed the land,
And of the nations doth defusion make;
The mountains rent, the hills for fear did quake:
His unknown paths no man may understand.

The Morians' tents, even for their wickedness,
I might behold, the land of Midian,
Amaz'd and trembling, like unto a man
Forsaken quite and left in great distress.

What, did the rivers move the Lord to ire?
Or did the floods his majesty displease?
Or was the Lord offended with the seas,
That thou camest forth in chariot hot as fire?

Thy force and power thou freely didst relate;
Unto the tribes thy oath doth surely stand;
And by thy strength thou didst divide the land,
And from the earth the rivers separate.

The mountains saw, and trembled for fear;
The sturdy stream with speed forth passed by;
The mighty depths shout out a hideous cry,
And then aloft their waves they did uprear.

The sun and moon amid their course stood still;
Thy spears and arrows forth with shining went:
Thou spoilest the land, being to anger bent,
And in displeasure thou didst slay and kill.

Thou wentest forth for thine own chosen's sake,
For the safeguard of thine anointed one:
The house of wicked men is overthrown,
And their foundations now go all to wrack.

Their towns thou strikest, by thy mighty power,
With their own weapons made for their defence,
Who like a whirlwind came with the pretence,
The poor and simple man quite to devour.

Thou madest thy horse on seas to gallop fast,
Upon the waves thou ridest here and there:
My entrails trembled then for very fear,
And at thy voice my lips shook at the last.

Grief pierced my bones, and fear did me annoy,
In time of trouble where I might find rest;
For to revenge when once the Lord is pressed,
With plagues he will the people quite destroy.

The fig tree now no more shall sprout nor flourish,
The pleasant vine no more with grapes abound;
No pleasure in the city shall be found,
The field no more her fruit shall feed nor nourish.

The sheep shall now be taken from the fold,
In stall of bullocks there shall be no choice:
Yet in the Lord, my Savior, I rejoice,
My hope in God yet will I surely hold.

God is my strength, the Lord my only stay;
My feet for swiftness it is he will make
Like to the hinds who none in course can take;
Upon high places he will make my way.

Another Song of the Faithful for the Mercies of God

Oh living Lord, I still will laud thy name!
    For though thou wert offended once with me,
Thy heavy wrath is turn'd from me again,
    And graciously thou now dost comfort me.

Behold, the Lord is my salvation;
    I trust in him, and fear not any power:
He is my song, the strength I lean upon;
    The Lord God is my loving Savior.

Therefore with joy out of the well of life
    Draw forth sweet water which it doth afford,
And in the day of trouble and of strife
    Call on the name of God, the living Lord:

Extol his works and wonders to the sun,
    Unto all people let his praise be shown,
Record in song the marvels he hath done,
    And let his glory through the world be blown.

Cry out aloud and shout on Sion hill;
    I give thee charge that this proclaimed be—
The great and mighty King of Israel
    Now only dwelleth in the midst of thee.

John Day (1566–1628)

Man's Natural Infirmity

What means my God? Why dost present to me
Such glorious objects? Can a blind man see?
Why dost thou call? Why dost thou beckon so?
Wouldst have me come? Lord, can cripple go?
Or, why dost thou expect that I should raise
Thy glory with my voice? the dumb can't praise.
Unscale my dusky eyes; then I'll express
Thy glorious object's strong attractiveness:
Dip thou my limbs in thy Bethesda's lake—
I'll scorn my earthly crutches; I'll forsake
Myself: touch thou my tongue, and then I'll sing
An hallelujah to my glorious King:
Raise me from this my grave—then I shall be
Alive, and I'll bestow my life on thee.
Till thou, Elijah-like, dost overspread
My limbs, I'm blind, I'm lame, I'm dumb—I'm dead!

John Donne (1572–1631)

"Thou hast made me, and shall thy work decay?"

Thou hast made me, and shall thy work decay?
Repair me now, for now mine end doth haste,
I run to death, and death meets me as fast,
And all my pleasures are like yesterday;

I dare not move my dim eyes any way,
Despair behind, and death before doth cast
Such terror, and my feeble flesh doth waste
By sin in it, which it t'wards hell doth weigh;
Only thou art above, and when towards thee
By thy leave I can look, I rise again;
But our old subtle foe so tempteth me,
That not one hour myself I can sustain;
Thy grace may wing me to prevent his art,
And thou like adamant draw mine iron heart.

"At the round earth's imagined corners, blow"

At the round earth's imagined corners, blow
Your trumpets, angels, and arise, arise
From death, you numberless infinities
Of souls, and to your scattered bodies go,
All whom the flood did, and the fire shall o'erthrow,
All whom war, dearth, age, agues, tyrannies,
Despair, law, chance, hath slain, and you whose eyes
Shall behold God, and never taste death's woe.
But let them sleep, Lord, and me mourn a space,
For, if above all these, my sins abound,
'Tis late to ask abundance of thy grace,
When we are there; here on this lowly ground,
Teach me how to repent; for that's as good
As if thou hadst sealed my pardon, with thy blood.

Ben Jonson (1574–1637)

Hymn to God the Father

Hear me, O God!
   A broken heart
   Is my best part:
Use still thy rod,
   That I may prove
   Therein thy love.

If thou hadst not
   Been stern to me,
   But left me free,
I had forgot
   Myself and thee.

For, sin's so sweet,
   As minds ill bent
   Rarely repent,
Until they meet
   Their punishment.
Who more can crave
   Than thou hast done?
   That gav'st a Son
To free a slave:
   First made of nought
   With all since bought.

Sin, death, and hell,
     His glorious name
     Quite overcame;
Yet I rebel,
     And slight the same.

But I'll come in,
     Before my loss
     Me further toss,
As sure to win
     Under his cross.

A Prayer

Good and great God! can I not think of thee,
But it must straight my melancholy be?
Is it interpreted in me disease,
That, laden with my sins, I seek for ease?
O be thou witness, that the reins dost know,
And hearts of all, if I be sad for show;
And judge me after, if I dare pretend
To aught but grace, or aim at other end.
As thou art all, so be thou all to me,
First, midst, and last, converted One and Three!
My faith, my hope, my love; and in this state,
My Judge, my Witness, and my Advocate.

Where have I been this while exiled from thee?
And whither rapt, now thou but stoop'st to me?
Dwell, dwell here still: O, being every where,
How can I doubt to find thee ever here?
I know my state both full of shame and scorn,
Conceived in sin, and unto labor born;
Standing with fear, and, must with horror fall,
And destined unto judgment after all.
I feel my griefs too; and there scarce is ground
Upon my flesh to inflict another wound;
Yet dare I not complain, or wish for death,
With holy Paul, lest it be thought the breath
Of discontent; or that these prayers be
For weariness of life, not love of thee.

To the Holy Trinity

I
O Holy, blessed, glorious Trinity
Of persons, still-one God in Unity.
The faithful man's believed mystery,
        Help, help to lift
Myself up to thee, harrow'd, torn, and bruised,
By sin and Satan; and my flesh misused,
As my heart lies in pieces, all confused,
        O take my gift.

II

All-gracious God, the sinner's sacrifice,
A broken heart, thou wert not wont despise;
But 'bove the fat of rams, or bulls to prize,
     An offering meet,
For thy acceptance: O, behold me right,
And take compassion on my grievous plight!
What odor can be, than a heart contrite,
     To thee more sweet?

III

Eternal Father, God, who didst create
This all of nothing, gav'st it form and fate,
And breath'st into it life and light, with state
     To worship thee.
Eternal God the Son, who not deniedst
To take our nature; becam'st man, and diedst,
To pay our debts, upon thy cross, and criedst
     ALL'S DONE IN ME.

IV

Eternal Spirit, God from both proceeding,
Father and Son; the Comforter, in breeding
Pure thoughts in man: with fiery zeal them feeding
     For acts of grace.
Increase those acts, O glorious Trinity
Of persons, still one God in Unity;
Till I attain the long'd-for mystery
     Of seeing your face.

V

Beholding one in three, and three in one,
A Trinity, to shine in Union;
The gladdest light dark man can think upon;
     O grant it me!
Father, and Son, and Holy Ghost, you three,
All co-eternal in your majesty,
Distinct in persons, yet in unity
     One God to see.

VI

My Maker, Saviour, and my Sanctifier!
To hear, to mediate, sweeten my desire
With grace, with love, with cherishing entire:
     O then how blest!
Among thy saints elected to abide,
And with thy angels placed, side by side,
But in thy presence, truly glorified
     Shall I there rest!

George Sandys (1577–1643)

Psalm 42

Lord! as the hart emboss'd with heat
Brays after the cool rivulet,
   So sighs my soul for thee.
My soul thirsts for the living God:

When shall I enter his abode,
   And there his beauty see?

Tears are my food both night and day;
While, Where's thy God? they daily say,
   My soul in plaints I shed;
When I remember, how in throngs
We fill'd thy house with praise and songs;
   How I their dances led.

My soul, why art thou so deprest?
Why, O! thus troubled in my breast,
   With grief so overthrown?
   With constant hope on God await:
I yet his name shall celebrate,
   For mercy timely shown?

My fainting heart within me pants:
My God, consider my complaints;
   My songs shall praise thee still.
Even from the vale where Jordan flows;
Where Hermon his high forehead shows,
   From Mitsar's humble hill.

Deeps unto deeps enraged call,
When thy dark spouts of waters fall,
   And dreadful tempest raves:
For all thy floods upon me burst,
And billows after billows thrust
   To swallow in their graves.

But yet by day the Lord will charge
His ready mercy to enlarge
   My soul, surprised with cares:
He gives my songs their argument;—
God of my life, I will present
   By night to thee my prayers:

And say, My God, my Rock, O why
Am I forgot, and mourning die,
   By foes reduc'd to dust?
Their words like weapons pierce my bones;
While still they echo to my groans,
   Where is the Lord thy trust?

My soul, why art thou so deprest!
O why so troubled in my breast!
   Sunk underneath thy load!
With constant hope on God await:
For I his name shall celebrate;
   My Saviour and my God.

Psalm 66

Happy sons of Israel,
Who in pleasant Canaan dwell,
Fill the air with shouts of joy;
Shouts redoubled from the sky.
Sing the great Jehovah's praise;
Trophies to his glory raise;

Say, How wonderful thy deeds!
Lord, thy power all power exceeds!
Conquest on thy sword doth sit;
Trembling foes through fear submit.
Let the many-peopled earth,
All of high and humble birth,
Worship our eternal King;
Hymns unto his honour sing.
Come, and see what God hath wrought;
Terrible to human thought!
He the billows did divide;
Wall'd with waves on either side,
While we passed safe and dry:
Then our soul were rapt with joy.
Endless his dominion;
All beholding from his throne.
Let not those who hate us most,
Let not the rebellious boast.
Bless the Lord; his praise be sung,
While an ear can hear a tongue.
He our feet establisheth;
He our souls redeems from death.
Lord, as silver purified,
Thou hast with affliction tried:
Thou hast driven into the net;
Burdens on our shoulders set:
Trod on by their horses' hooves;
Theirs, whom pity never moves.
We through fire, with flames embrac'd,
We through raging floods have pass'd:

Yet by thy conducting hand,
Brought into a wealthy land.
I will to thy house repair;
Worship, and thy power declare:
Offerings on thy altar lay;
All my vows devoutly pay,
Utter'd with my heart and tongue,
When oppress'd with powerful wrong.
Fatlings I will sacrifice;
Incense in perfume shall rise;
Bullocks, shaggy goats, and rams
Offered up in sacred flames.
You, who great Jehovah fear,
Come, O come, you bless'd, and hear
What for me the Lord hath wrought,
Then, when near to ruin brought.
Fervently to him I cried;
I his goodness magnified.
If I vices should affect,
Would not he my prayers reject?
But the Lord my prayers hath heard,
Which my tongue with tears preferr'd.
Source of mercy, be thou blest,
That hast granted my request.

George Wither (1588–1667)

Divine Support

I should not care how hard my fortunes were,
Might still my hopes be such, as now they are,
Of help divine; nor fear how poor I be,
If thoughts yet present still may bide in me;
For they have left assurance of such aid,
That I am of no dangers now afraid.

    Yea, now I see, methinks, what weak and vain
Supporters I have sought, to help sustain
My fainting heart; when some injurious hand
Would undermine the station where I stand.
Methinks I see how scurvy, and how base
It is, to scrape for favors and for grace
To men of earthly minds, and unto those
Who may, perhaps, before to-morrow, lose
Their wealth, or their abus'd authority,
And stand as much in want of help as I.

    Methinks, in this new rapture I do see
The hand of God from heaven supporting me,
Without those rotten aids for which I whin'd
When I was of my other, vulgar mind;
And if in some one part of me it lay,
I now could cut that limb of me away.
Still might I keep this mind, there were enough
Within myself (beside that cumbrous stuff
We seek without) which, husbanded aright,
Would make me rich in all the world's despite;

And I have hopes, that had she quite bereft me
Of those few rags and toys, which yet are left me,
I should on God alone so much depend,
That I should need nor wealth, nor other friend.

Well-Doing

When to the fields we walk, to look upon
Some skilful marksman, so much heed we not
How many arrows from his bow are gone,
As we observe how nigh the mark he shot;
And justly we deride that man who spends
His time and shafts, but never aim doth take
To hit the white, or foolishly pretends
The number of the shots doth archers make.
So God, who marketh our endeavours here,
Doth not by tale account of them receive;
But heedeth rather how well-meant they were,
And at his will how rightly aim'd we have.
   It is not mumbling over, thrice a day,
A set of *Ave Maries* or of creeds,
Or many hours formally to pray,
When from a dull devotion it proceeds;
Nor is it up and down the land to seek,
To find those well-breath'd lecturers, that can
Preach thrice a sabbath, and six times a week,
Yet be as fresh as when they first began:
Nor is it such-like things, performed by number,
Which God respects; nor doth his wisdom crave
Those many vanities, wherewith some cumber

Their bodies, as if those their souls could save.
For not much-doing, but well-doing, that
Which God commands, the doer justifies.
To pray without devotion is to prate;
And hearing is but half our exercise:
We ought not, therefore, to regard, alone,
How often, but how well, the work be done.

⟨∽⟩

Henry King (1591–1669)

A Penitential Hymne

Hearken, O God, unto a Wretch's cries.
Who low dejected at thy footstool lies.
Let not the clamour of my heinous sin
Drown my requests, which strive to enter in
At those bright gates, which always open stand
To such as beg remission at thy hand.

Too well I know, if thou in rigour deal
I can nor pardon ask, nor yet appeal:
To my hoarse voice, heaven will no audience grant,
But deaf as brass, and hard as adamant
Beat back my words; therefore I bring to thee
A gracious *Advocate* to plead for me.

What though my leprous soul no *Jordan* can
Recure, nor floods of the lav'd Ocean
Make clean? yet from my Saviour's bleeding side
Two large and medicinable rivers glide.
Lord, wash me where those streams of life abound,
And new *Bethesdas* flow from ev'ry wound.

If I this precious Lather may obtain,
I shall not then despair for any stain;
I need no *Gilead's* balm, nor oil, nor shall
I for the purifying Hyssop call:
My spots will vanish in *His* purple flood,
And *crimson* there turn *white*, though washt with blood.

See Lord! with broken heart and bended knee,
How I address my humble suit to Thee;
O give that suit admittance to thy ears
Which floats to thee not in my words but tears:
And let my sinful soul this mercy crave
Before I fall into the silent grave.

Robert Herrick (1591–1674)

Neutrality Loathsome

God will have all, or none; serve Him, or fall
Down before Baal, Bel, or Belial:
Either be hot, or cold: God doth despise,
Abhorre, and spew out all Neutralities.

To God, on His Sicknesse

What though my Harp, and Viol be
Both hung upon the Willow-tree?
What though my bed be now my grave,
And for my house I darkness have?
What though my healthful days are fled,
And I lie numbered with the dead?
Yet I have hope, by Thy great power,
To spring; though now a wither'd flower.

Litany to the Holy Spirit

In the hour of my distress,
When temptations me oppress,
And when I my sins confess,
    Sweet Spirit, comfort me.

When I lie within my bed,
Sick in heart and sick in head,
And with doubts disquieted,
    Sweet Spirit, comfort me.

When the house doth sigh and weep,
And the world is drown'd in sleep,
Yet mine eyes the watch do keep,
    Sweet Spirit, comfort me.

When the passing-bell doth toll,
And the furies, in a shoal
Come to fright my parting soul,
   Sweet Spirit, comfort me.

When the priest his last hath pray'd,
And I nod to what is said,
'Cause my speech is now decay'd,
   Sweet Spirit, comfort me.

When, God knows, I'm toss'd about,
Either with despair or doubt,
Yet before the glass be out,
   Sweet Spirit, comfort me.

When the Tempter me pursu'th
With the sins of all my youth,
And half-damns me with untruth,
   Sweet Spirit, comfort me.

When the flames and hellish cries
Fright mine ears and fright mine eyes,
And all terrors me surprise,
   Sweet Spirit, comfort me.

When the judgment is reveal'd,
And that open'd which was seal'd,
When to Thee I have appeal'd,
   Sweet Spirit, comfort me.

Francis Quarles (1592–1664)

"Why dost thou shade thy lovely face?"

Why dost thou shade thy lovely face? O why
Does that eclipsing hand so long deny
The sunshine of thy soul-enlivening eye?

Without that light, what light remains in me?
Thou art my life, my way, my light; in thee
I live, I move, and by thy beams I see:

Thou art my life; if thou but turn away,
My life's a thousand deaths: thou art my way;
Without thee, Lord, I travel not, but stray:

My light thou art; without thy glorious sight,
Mine eyes are darkened with perpetual night:
My God, thou art my way, my life, my light.

Thou art my way; I wander if thou fly:
Thou art my light; if hid, how blind am I!
Thou art my life; if thou withdraw, I die.

Mine eyes are blind and dark, I cannot see;
To whom or whither should my darkness flee,
But to the light? and who's that light but thee?

My path is lost, my wandering steps do stray;
I cannot safely go, nor safely stay;
Whom should I seek but thee, my path, my way?

Oh, I am dead: to whom shall I, poor I,
Repair? to whom shall my sad ashes fly
But life? and where is life but in thine eye?

And yet thou turn'st away thy face, and fliest me;
And yet I sue for grace, and thou deniest me;
Speak, art thou angry, Lord, or only triest me?

Unscreen those heavenly lamps, or tell me why
Thou shad'st thy face: perhaps thou think'st no eye
Can view those flames, and not drop down and die.

If that be all, shine forth, and draw thee nigher;
Let me behold and die, for my desire
Is phoenix-like to perish in that fire.

Death-conquered Lazarus was redeemed by thee:
If I am dead, Lord, set death's prisoner free;
Am I more spent or stink I worse than he?

If my puffed life be out, give leave to tine
My shameless snuff at that bright lamp of thine:
Oh what's thy light the less for lighting mine?

If I have lost my path, great Shepherd, say,
Shall I still wander in a doubtful way?
Lord, shall a lamb of Israel's sheepfold stray?

Thou art the pilgrim's path, the blind man's eye,
The dead man's life: on thee my hopes rely;
If thou remove, I err, I grope, I die.

Disclose thy sunbeams, close thy wings, and stay;
See, see how I am blind, and dead, and stray,
O thou that art my light, my life, my way.

Delight in God Only

I love (and have some cause to love) the earth:
She is my Maker's creature; therefore good:
She is my mother, for she gave me birth;
She is my tender nurse; she gives me food;
    But what's a creature, Lord, compar'd with thee?
    Or what's my mother, or my nurse to me?

I love the air: her dainty sweets refresh
My drooping soul, and to new sweets invite me;
Her shrill-mouth'd quire sustains me with their flesh,
And with their polyphonian notes delight me:
    But what's the air or all the sweets that she
    Can bless my soul withal, compared to thee?

I love the sea: she is my fellow-creature,
My careful purveyor; she provides me store:
She walls me round; she makes my diet greater;
She wafts my treasure from a foreign shore:
    But, Lord of oceans, when compar'd with thee,
    What is the ocean, or her wealth to me?

To heav'n's high city I direct my journey,
Whose spangled suburbs entertain mine eye;
Mine eye, by contemplation's great attorney,
Transcends the crystal pavement of the sky:
 But, what is heav'n, great God, compar'd to thee?
 Without thy presence heav'n's no heaven to me.

Without thy presence earth gives no refection;
Without thy presence sea affords no treasure;
Without thy presence air's a rank infection;
Without thy presence heav'n itself no pleasure:
 If not possess'd, if not enjoy'd in thee,
 What's earth, or sea, or air, or heav'n to me?

The highest honor, that the world can boast,
Are subjects far too low for my desire;
The brightest beams of glory are (at most)
But dying sparkles of thy living fire:
 The loudest flames that earth can kindle, be
 But nightly glow-worms if compar'd to thee.

Without thy presence, wealth is bags of cares;
Wisdom, but folly; joy, disquiet—sadness:
Friendship is treason, and delights are snares;
Pleasures but pain, and mirth but pleasing madness:
 Without thee, Lord, things be not what they be,
 Nor have they being, when compar'd with thee.

In having all things, and not thee, what have I?
Not having thee, what have my labours got?
Let me enjoy but thee, what further crave I?
And having thee alone, what have I not?
    I wish nor sea, nor land; nor would I be
    Possess'd of heav'n, heav'n unpossess'd of thee.

Man's Ingratitude

A thankful heart hath earn'd one favor twice,
But he that is ungrateful, wants no vice:
The beast, that only lives the life of sense,
Prone to his several actions, and propense
To what he does, without the advice of will,
Guided by nature (that does nothing ill),
In practick maxims, proves it a thing hateful,
To accept a favor, and to live ungrateful:
But man, whose more diviner soul hath gain'd
A higher step to reason; nay, attain'd
A higher step than that, the light of grace,
Comes short of them, and in that point more base
Than they, most prompt and versed in that rude,
Unnatural, and high sin, ingratitude.
The stall-fed ox, that is grown fat, will know
His careful feeder, and acknowledge too;
The prouder stallion will at length espy
His master's bounty in his keeper's eye;
The air-dividing falcon will requite
Her falc'ner's pains with a well-pleasing flight;

The generous spaniel loves his master's eye;
And licks his fingers, though no meat be by:
But man, ungrateful man, that's born and bred
By heaven's immediate pow'r; maintain'd and fed
By his providing hand; observ'd, attended
By his indulgent grace; preserv'd, defended
By his prevailing arm: this man, I say,
Is more ungrateful, more obdure than they.
By him we live and move, from him we have
What blessings he can give, or we can crave:
Food for our hunger, dainties for our pleasure;
Trades for our business; pastimes for our leisure.
In grief, he is our joy; in want, our wealth;
In bondage, freedom; and in sickness, health;
In peace, our council; and in war, our leader;
At sea, our pilot; and in suits, our pleader;
In pain, our help; in triumph, our renown;
In life, our comfort; and in death, our crown:
Yet man, O most ungrateful man, can ever
Enjoy thy gift, but never mind the giver;
And like the swine, though pamper'd with enough,
His eyes are never higher than the trough.
We still receive; our hearts we seldom lift
To heaven; but drown the giver in the gift;
We taste the scollops, and return the shells—
Our sweet pomegranates want their silver bells:
We take the gift; the hand that did present it
We oft reward; forget the friend that sent it.

A blessing given to those will not disburse
Some thanks, is little better than a curse.
Great giver of all blessings, thou that art
The Lord of gifts, give me a grateful heart:
O give me that, or keep thy favours from me!
I wish no blessings with a vengeance to me.

A Soliloquy

Where shall I find my God? O where, O where,
Shall I direct my steps to find him there?
Shall I make search in swelling bags of coin?
Ah! no; for God and Mammon cannot join.
Do beds of down contain this heavenly stranger?
No, no, he's rather cradled in some manger:
Dwells he in wisdom? is he gone that road?
No, no, man's wisdom's foolishness with God:
Or hath some new plantation yet unknown,
Made him their king, adorn'd him with their crown?
No, no; the kingdoms of the earth think scorn
To adorn his brows with any crown but thorn.
Where shall I go to trace, where go to wind him?
My Lord is gone; and O! I cannot find him:
I'll ransack the dark dungeons; I'll inquire
Into the furnace, after the seventh fire:
I'll seek in Daniel's den, and in Paul's prison;
I'll search his grave, and see if he be risen:
I'll go to the house of mourning; and I'll call
At every alms-abused hospital:

I'll go and ask the widow that's opprest;
The heavy-laden that inquireth rest.
I'll search the corners of all broken hearts;
The wounded conscience, and the soul that smarts;
The contrite spirit fill'd with filial fear—
Ay, there he is; and nowhere else but there:
Spare not to scourge thy pleasure, O my God,
So I may find thy presence with thy rod.

Trial Before Reward

What joyful harvester did e'er obtain
The sweet fruition of his hopeful gain,
Till he in hardy labors first had pass'd
The summer's heat, and stormy winter's blast?
A sable night returns a shining morrow,
And days of joy ensue sad nights of sorrow;
The way to bliss lies not on beds of down,
And he that had no cross deserves no crown.
There's but one heaven, one place of perfect ease,
In man it lies, to take it where he please,
Above, or here below: and few men do
Enjoy the one, and taste the other too:
Sweating, and constant labor wins the goal
Of rest; afflictions clarify the soul,
And like hard masters, give more hard directions,
Tutoring the nonage of uncurb'd affections.
Wisdom, the antidote of sad despair,
Make sharp afflictions seem not as they are,

Through patient sufferance; and doth apprehend,
Not as they seeming are, but as they end.
To bear affliction with a bended brow,
Or stubborn heart, is but to disallow
The speedy means to health; salve heals no sore,
If misapplied, but makes the grief the more.
Who sends affliction, sends an end, and he
Best knows what's best for him, what's best for me:
'Tis not for me to carve me where I like;
Him pleases when he list to stroke or strike.
I'll neither wish nor yet avoid temptation,
But still expect it, and make preparation:
If he think best, my faith shall not be tried,
Lord, keep me spotless from presumptuous pride:
If otherwise with his trial, give me care,
By thankful patience to prevent despair:
Fit me to bear whate'er thou shalt assign;
I kiss the rod, because the rod is thine.
    Howe'er, let me not boast, nor yet repine,
    With trial, or without, Lord, make me thine.

On Man's Two Enemies

Two potent enemies attend on man,
One's fat and plump, the other lean and wan.
The one fawns and smiles, the other weeps as fast;
The first Presumption is, Despair the last:
That feeds upon the bounty of full treasure,
Brings jolly news of peace, and lasting pleasure;

This feeds on want, unapt to entertain
God's blessings; finds them ever in the wane.
Their maxims disagree; but their conclusion
Is the self-same; both jump in man's confusion.
Lord, keep me from the first, or else I shall
Soar up and melt my waxen wings and fall:
Lord, keep the second from me; lest I then
Sink down so low, I never rise again:
Teach me to know myself, and what I am,
And my presumption will be turned to shame:
Give me true faith to know thy dying Son,
What ground has then despair to work upon?
To avoid my shipwreck upon either shelf,
O, teach me, Lord, to know my God—myself.

◦◦

George Herbert (1593–1632)

Denial

When my devotions could not pierce
Thy silent ears,
Then was my heart broken, as was my verse;
My breast was full of fears
And disorder;

My bent thoughts, like a brittle bow,
Did fly asunder;
Each took his way; some would to pleasures go,
Some to the wars and thunder
Of alarms.

As good go any where, they say,
As to benumb
Both knees and heart in crying night and day,
"Come, come, my God, O come!"
But no hearing.

O that Thou shouldst give dust a tongue
To cry to Thee,
And then not hear it crying! All day long
My heart was in my knee,
But no hearing.

Therefore my soul lay out of sight,
Untun'd, unstrung;
My feeble spirit, unable to look right,
Like a nipt blossom, hung
Discontented.

O, cheer and tune my heartless breast,
Defer no time;
That so Thy favors granting my request,
They and my soul may chime,
And mend my rhyme.

The Flower

How fresh, O Lord, how sweet and clean
Are thy returns! ev'n as the flow'rs in spring:
To which, besides their own demean,
The late-past frost's tributes of pleasure bring.

Grief melts away
Like snow in May,
As if there were no such cold thing.

Who would have thought my shrivell'd heart
Could have recover'd greenness? It was gone
Quite under ground, as flowers depart
To see their mother-root, when they have blown;
Where they together
All the hard weather
Dead to the world, keep house unknown.

These are thy wonders, Lord of power!
Killing and quick'ning, bringing down to hell
And up to heaven in an hour;
Making a chiming of a passing-bell.
We say amiss,
"This or that is:"
Thy word is all, if we would spell.

Oh, that I once past changing were;
Fast in thy Paradise, where no flow'r can wither!
Many a spring I shot up fair,
Offering at heav'n, growing and groaning thither:
Nor doth my flower
Want a spring-shower,
My sins and I joining together.

But, while I grow in a straight line,
Still upwards bent, as if heav'n were mine own,

Thy anger comes, and I decline:
What frost to that? What pole is not the zone
   Where all things burn,
   When thou dost turn,
And the least frown of thine is shown?

   And now in age I bud again;
After so many deaths I live and write,
  I once more smell the dew and rain,
And relish versing. O my only light,
   It cannot be
   That I am he,
On whom thy tempests fell all night!

These are thy wonders, Lord of love!
To make us see we are but flow'rs that glide:
  Which when we once can find and prove,
Thou hast a garden for us, where to 'bide.
   Who would be more,
   Swelling through store,
Forfeit their Paradise by their pride.

Faith

  Lord, how couldst thou so much appease
Thy wrath for sin, as, when man's sight was dim,
And could see little, to regard his ease,
  And bring by faith all things to him?

Hungry I was, and had no meat,
I did conceit a most delicious feast;
I had it straight, and did as truly eat,
  As ever did a welcome guest.

There is a rare outlandish root,
Which when I could not get, I thought it here:
That apprehension cur'd so well my foot,
  That I can walk to heav'n well near.

I owed thousands, and much more:
I did believe that I did nothing owe,
And liv'd accordingly; my creditor
  Believes so too, and lets me go.

Faith makes me any thing, or all,
That I believe is in the sacred story:
And when sin placeth me in Adam's fall,
  Faith sets me higher in his glory.

If I go lower in the book,
What can be lower than the common manger?
Faith puts me there with him, who sweetly took
  Our flesh and frailty, death and danger.

If bliss had lien in art or strength,
None but the wise and strong had gained it:
Where now, by faith, all arms are of a length;
  One size doth all conditions fit.

A peasant may believe as much
As a great clerk, and reach the highest stature.
Thus dost thou make proud knowledge bend and crouch,
    While grace fills up uneven nature.

When creatures had no real light
Inherent in them, thou didst make the sun
Impute a lustre, and allow them bright;
    And in this show what Christ hath done.

That which before was darkn'd clean,
With bushy groves, pricking the looker's eye,
Vanish'd away, when faith did change the scene;
    And then appear'd a glorious sky.

What though my body run to dust?
Faith cleaves unto it, counting ev'ry grain,
With an exact and most particular trust,
Reserving all for flesh again.

The Temper

How should I praise thee, Lord! how should my rhymes
    Gladly engrave thy love in steel,
If what my soul doth feel sometimes,
    My soul might ever feel!

Although there were some forty heav'ns, or more,
　　Sometimes I peer above them all;
　　Sometimes I hardly reach a score;
　　　　Sometimes to hell I fall.

O rack me not to such a vast extent;
　　Those distances belong to thee:
　　The world's too little for thy tent,
　　　　A grave too big for me.

Wilt thou meet arms with man, that thou dost stretch
　　A crumb of dust from heav'n to hell?
　　Will great God measure with a wretch?
　　　　Shall he thy stature spell?

O let me, when thy roof my soul hath hid,
　　O let me roost and nestle there:
　　Then of a sinner thou art rid,
　　　　And I of hope and fear.

Yet take thy way; for sure thy way is best:
　　Stretch or contract me, thy poor debtor:
　　This is but tuning of my breast,
　　　　To make the music better.

Whether I fly with angels, fall with dust,
　　Thy hands made both, and I am there.
　　Thy power and love, my love and trust
　　　　Make one place everywhere.

The Holy Scriptures

I

Oh Book! infinite sweetness! let my heart
    Suck every letter, and a honey gain
    Precious for any grief in any part,
To clear the breast, to mollify all pain.

Thou art all health, health thriving till it make
    A full eternity: thou art a mass
    Of strange delights, where we may wish and take.
Ladies, look here; this is the thankful glass,

That mends the looker's eyes: this is the well
    That washes what it shows. Who can endear
    Thy praise too much? thou art heaven's lieger here,

Working against the states of death and hell.
    Thou art joy's handsel: heaven lies flat in thee,
    Subject to every mounter's bended knee.

II

Oh that I knew how all thy lights combine,
And the configurations of their glory!
Seeing not only how each verse doth shine,
But all the constellations of the story.

This verse marks that, and both do make a motion
Unto a third, that ten leaves off doth lie.
Then, as dispersed herbs do watch a potion,
These three make up some Christian's destiny.

Such are thy secrets, which my life makes good,
And comments on thee: for in ev'ry thing
Thy words do find me out, and parallels bring,
And in another make me understood.

Stars are poor books, and oftentimes do miss:
This book of stars lights to eternal bliss.

The Collar

I struck the board, and cried, "No more!
    I will abroad,
  What! shall I ever sigh and pine?
My lines and life are free; free as the road,
  Loose as the wind, as large as store.
    Shall I be still in suit?
  Have I no harvest, but a thorn
To let me blood; and not restore
What I have lost with cordial fruit?
    Sure there was wine,
  Before my sighs did dry it: there was corn,
    Before my tears did drown it.
  Is the year only lost to *me*?
    Have I no bays to crown it?
No flowers, no garlands gay? all blasted?
    All wasted?
  Not so, my heart! but there is fruit,
      And thou hast hands.
      Recover all thy sigh-blown age

On double pleasures: leave thy cold dispute
Of what is fit, and not. Forsake thy cage,
     Thy rope of sands,
Which petty thoughts have made, and made to thee
Good cable; to enforce and draw,
     And be thy law;
  While thou didst wink and wouldst not see.
     Away; take heed!
     I will abroad,
Call in thy death's-head there: tie up thy fears.
     He, that forbears
     To suit and serve his need,
     Deserves his load."
But as I rav'd, and grew more fierce and wild
     At every word,
  Methought I heard one calling, "Child!"
And I replied, "My Lord!"

Christopher Harvey (1597–1663)

Confusion

O! How my mind.
     Is gravel'd!
          Not a thought
That I can find
     But's ravel'd
          All to nought.

Short ends of threads,
   And narrow shreds,
     Of lists,
Knots snarled ruffs,
   Loose broken tufts
     Of twists,
Are my torn meditation's ragged clothing,
Which wound, and woven shape a suit for nothing:
One while I think, and then I am in pain
To think how to unthink that thought again.
How can my soul
   But famish
     With this food?
Pleasure's full bowl
   Tastes rammish,
     Taints the blood.
Profit picks bones,
   And chews on stones
     That choke.
Honor climbs hills,
   Fats not, but fills
     With smoke.
And whilst my thoughts are greedy upon these
They pass by pearls, and stoop to pick up peas,
Such wash and dross is fit for none but swine:
And such I am not, Lord, if I am thine.
 Clothe me now, and feed me then afresh:
 Else my soul dies famish't, and starv'd with flesh.

Comfort in Extremity

Alas! my Lord is going,
　　　　Oh my woe!
It will be mine undoing;
　　　　If he go
I'll run and overtake him:
　　　　If he stay
I'll cry aloud, and make him
　　　　Look this way:
　　O stay, my Lord, my love, 'tis I,
　　Comfort me quickly, or I die.

Cheer up thy drooping spirits
　　　　I am here.
Mine all-sufficient merits
　　　　Shall appear
Before the throne of glory
　　　　In thy stead:
I'll put into the story
　　　　What I did,
　　Lift up thine eyes, sad soul, and see
　　Thy Saviour here. Lo, I am he.

Alas! shall I present
　　　　My sinfulness
To thee? Thou wilt resent
　　　　The loathsomeness.

Be not afraid, I'll take
　　　　Thy sins on me,

> *And all my favor make*
> > *To shine on thee.*

> Lord what thou'lt have me, thou must make me.

> *As I have made thee now, I take thee.*

⁓

Thomas Heywood (d. 1641)

Search after God

I sought thee round about, O thou my God!
> In thine abode.
I said unto the earth, "Speak, art thou he?"
> She answer'd me,
"I am not."—I enquired of creatures all,
> In general,
Contain'd therein;—they with one voice proclaim,
That none amongst them challenged such a name.

I ask'd the seas, and all the deeps below,
> My God to know.
I ask'd the reptiles, and whatever is
> In the abyss;
Even from the shrimp to the leviathan
> Enquiry ran:
But in those deserts which no line can sound,
The God I sought for was not to be found.

I ask'd the air, if that were he? but,
  It told me *No.*
I from the towering eagle to the wren,
  Demanded then,
If any feather'd fowl 'mongst them were such?
  But they all, much
Offended with my question, in full quire,
Answered, "To find thy God thou must look higher."

I ask'd the heavens, sun, moon, and stars, but they
  Said, "We obey
The God thou seek'st."—I ask'd, what eye or ear
  Could see or hear;
What in the world I might descry or know
  Above, below:
—With an unanimous voice, all these things said,
"We are not God, but we by him were made."

I ask'd the world's great universal mass,
  If that God was?
Which was a mighty and strong voice replied,
  As stupified,
"I am not he, O man! for know that I,
  By him on high,
Was fashion'd first of nothing, thus instated,
And sway'd by him, by whom I was created."

I sought the court; but smooth-tongued flattery there
  Deceived each ear:

In the throng'd city there was selling, buying,
      Swearing, and lying;
I'the country, craft in simpleness array'd:
      And then I said,
"Vain is my search, although my pains be great—
Where my God is there can be no deceit."

A scrutiny within myself I, then,
      Even thus began:
"O man, what art thou?"—What more could I say,
      Than dust and clay?
Frail, mortal, fading, a mere puff, a blast;
      That cannot last;
Enthroned to-day, to-morrow in an urn;
Form'd from that earth to which I must return.

I ask'd myself, what this great God might be
      That fashion'd me?
I answer'd—the all-potent, solely immense,
      Surpassing sense;
Unspeakable, inscrutable, eternal,
      Lord over all;
The only terrible, strong, just, and true,
Who hath no end, and no beginning knew.

He is the well of life, for he doth give
      To all that live,
Both breath and being: he is the Creator
      Both of the water,

Earth, air, and fire. Of all things that subsist,
    He hath the list;
Of all the heavenly host, or what earth claims,
He keeps the scroll, and calls them by their names.

And now, my God, by thine illumining grace,
    Thy glorious face
(So far forth as it may discover'd be)
    Methinks I see;
And though invisible and infinite—
    To human sight,
Thou, in thy mercy, justice, truth, appearest,
In which to our weak senses thou comest nearest.

O make us apt to seek, and quick to find,
    Thou God, most kind!
Give us love, hope and faith in thee to trust,
    Thou God, most just!
Remit all our offences, we intreat;
    Most Good, most Great!
Grant that our willing, though unworthy quest
May, through thy grace, admit us 'mongst the blest.

Thomas Washbourne (1606–1687)

Casting All Your Care upon God, for He Careth for You

I Peter 5:7

Come heavy souls, oppressed that are,
With doubts, and fears, and carking care.
Lay all your burdens down and see
Where's one that carried once a tree
Upon his back, and which is more,
A heavier weight, your sins he bore.
Think then how easily he can
Your sorrows bear that's God and Man;
Think too how willing he's to take
Your care on him, who for your sake
Sweat bloody drops, prayed, fasted, cried,
Was bound, scourged, mocked, and crucified.
He that so much for you did do,
Will yet do more, and care for you.

∽

John Milton (1608–1687)

On His Blindness

When I consider how my light is spent,
　　Ere half my days, in this dark world and wide,
　　And that one talent which is death to hide,
　　Lodg'd with me useless, though my soul more bent

To serve therewith my Maker, and present
   My true account, lest he returning chide;
   "Doth God exact day-labor, light denied?"
   I fondly ask. But Patience, to prevent
That murmur, soon replies, "God doth not need
   Either man's work or his own gifts; who best
   Bear his mild yoke, they serve him best; his state
Is kingly. Thousands at his bidding speed
   And post o'er land and ocean without rest;
   They also serve who only stand and wait.

Abraham Cowley (1618–1667)

Reason: The Use of It in Divine Matters

Some blind themselves, 'cause possibly they may
   Be led by others a right way;
They build on sands, which if unmov'd they find,
   'Tis but because there was no wind.
Less hard 'tis not to err ourselves, than know
   If our forefathers err'd or no.
When we trust men concerning God, we then
   Trust not God concerning men.

Visions and inspirations some expect,
   Their course here to direct.
Like senseless chymists their own wealth destroy,
   Imaginary gold to enjoy.

So stars appear to drop to us from sky,
  And gild the passage as they fly;
But when they fall, and meet the opposing ground,
  What but a sordid slime is found?

Sometimes their fancies they 'bove reason set,
  And fast, that they may dream of meat.
Sometimes ill spirits their sickly souls delude;
  And bastard forms obtrude.
So Endor's wretched sorceress, although
  She Saul through his disguise did know,
Yet when the devil comes up disguis'd, she cries,
  "Behold, the gods arise!"

In vain, alas! these outward hopes are tried;
  Reason within's our only guide.
Reason which (God be prais'd) still walks, for all
  Its old original fall.
And since itself the boundless Godhead join'd
  With a reasonable mind,
It plainly shows that mysteries divine
  May with our reason join.

The holy book, like the eighth sphere, does shine
  With thousand lights of truth divine:
So numberless the stars, that to the eye
  It makes but all one galaxy.
Yet reason must assist too, for in seas
  So vast and dangerous as these,

Our course by stars above we cannot know,
    Without the compass too below.

Though reason cannot through faith's myst'ries see,
    It sees that there and such they be;
Leads to heav'n's door, and there does humbly keep,
    And there through chinks and key-holes peep.
Though it, like Moses, by a sad command
    Must not come into th' Holy Land,
Yet thither it infallibly does guide,
    And from afar 'tis all descried.

∼∂

Andrew Marvell (1621–1678)

On a Drop of Dew

See, how the orient dew
    Shed from the bosom of the morn
    Into the blowing roses
    (Yet careless of its mansion new,
For the clear region where 'twas born),
    Round in itself incloses;
    And, in its little globe's extent,
Frames, as it can, its native element.
    How it the purple flower does slight,
    Scarce touching where it lies;
    But gazing back upon the skies,
    Shines with a mournful light,
    Like its own tear,

Because so long divided from the sphere.
   Restless it rolls, and unsecure,
     Trembling, lest it grow impure;
   Till the warm sun pity its pain,
And to the skies exhale it back again.
    So the soul, that drop, that ray
Of the clear fountain of eternal day
(Could it within the human flower be seen),
   Remembering still its former height,
   Shuns the sweet leaves, and blossoms green
   And, recollecting its own light,
Does, in its pure and circling thoughts, express
The greater heaven in an heaven less.
      In how coy a figure wound,
      Every way it turns away;
      So the world-excluding round,
      Yet receiving in the day;
      Dark beneath, but bright above,
      Here disdaining, there in love.
   How loose and easy hence to go;
   How girt and ready to ascend;
   Moving but on a point below,
   It all about does upwards bend.
Such did the manna's sacred dew distil;
White and entire, though congealed and chill;
Congealed on earth; but does, dissolving, run
Into the glories of the almighty sun.

Henry Vaughan (1622–1695)

The Pursuit

Lord! what a busy, restless thing
    Hast thou made man?
Each day, and hour he is on wing,
    Rests not a span;
Then having lost the Sun, and light
    By clouds surpris'd
He keeps a Commerce in the night
    With air disguis'd;
Hadst thou given to this active dust
    A state untir'd,
The lost Son had not left the husk
    Nor home desir'd;
That was thy secret, and it is
    Thy mercy too,
For when all fails to bring to bliss,
    Then, this must do.
Ah! Lord! and what a Purchase will that be
To take us sick, that sound would not take thee?

"They are all gone into the world of light!"

They are all gone into the world of light!
    And I alone sit ling'ring here;
Their very memory is fair and bright,
    And my sad thoughts doth clear.

It glows and glitters in my cloudy breast
　　Like stars upon some gloomy grove,
Or those faint beams in which this hill is drest,
　　After the Sun's remove.

I see them walking in an Air of glory,
　　Whose light doth trample on my days:
My days, which are at best but dull and hoary,
　　Mere glimmering and decays.

O holy hope! and high humility,
　　High as the Heavens above!
These are your walks, and you have shew'd them me
　　To kindle my cold love,

Dear, beauteous death! the Jewel of the Just,
　　Shining no where, but in the dark;
What mysteries do lie beyond thy dust;
　　Could man outlook that mark!

He that hath found some fledg'd bird's nest, may know
　　At first sight, if the bird be flown;
But what fair Well, or Grove he sings in now,
　　That is to him unknown.

And yet, as Angels in some brighter dreams
　　Call to the soul, when man doth sleep:
So some strange thoughts transcend our wonted themes,
　　And into glory peep.

If a star were confin'd into a Tomb
   Her captive flames must needs burn there;
But when the hand that lockt her up, gives room,
   She'll shine through all the sphere.

O Father of eternal life, and all
     Created glories under thee!
Resume thy spirit from this world of thrall
     Into true liberty.

Either disperse these mists, which blot and fill
     My perspective (still) as they pass,
Or else remove me hence unto that hill,
     Where I shall need no glass.

Cock-crowing

Father of lights! what Sunny seed,
What glance of day hast thou confin'd
Into this bird? To all the breed
This busy Ray thou hast assign'd;
     Their magnetism works all night,
     And dreams of Paradise and light.

Their eyes watch for the morning hue,
Their little grain expelling night
So shines and sings, as if it knew
The path unto the house of light.
     It seems their candle, howe'r done,
     Was tinn'd and lighted at the sun.

If such a tincture, such a touch,
So firm a longing can impower,
Shall thy own image think it much
To watch for thy appearing hour?
    If a mere blast so fill the sail,
    Shall not the breath of God prevail?

O thou immortal light and heat!
Whose hand so shines through all this frame,
That by the beauty of the seat,
We plainly see, who made the same.
    Seeing thy seed abides in me,
    Dwell thou in it, and I in thee.

To sleep without thee, is to die;
Yea, 'tis a death partakes of hell:
For where thou dost not close the eye
It never opens, I can tell.
    In such a dark, Egyptian border,
    The shades of death dwell and disorder.

If joys, and hopes, and earnest throws,
And hearts, whose Pulse beats still for light
Are given to birds; who, but thee, knows
A love-sick soul's exalted flight?
    Can souls be track'd by any eye
    But his, who gave them wings to fly?

Only this Veil which thou hast broke,
And must be broken yet in me,

This veil, I say, is all the cloak
And cloud which shadows thee from me.
 This veil thy full-ey'd love denies,
 And only gleams and fractions spies.

O take it off! make no delay,
But brush me with thy light, that I
May shine unto a perfect day,
And warm me at thy glorious Eye!
 O take it off! or till it flee,
 Though with no Lily, stay with me!

The Water-fall

With what deep murmurs through time's silent stealth
Doth, thy transparent, cool and wat'ry wealth
 Here flowing fall,
 And chide, and call,
As if his liquid, loose Retinue stayed
Ling'ring, and were of this steep place afraid,
 The common pass
 Where, clear as glass,
 All must descend
 Not to an end:
But quick'ned by this deep and rocky grave,
Rise to a longer course more bright and brave.

 Dear stream! dear bank, where often I
 Have sat, and pleas'd my pensive eye,

Why, since each drop of thy quick store
Runs thither, whence it flow'd before,
Should poor souls fear a shade or night,
Who came (sure) from a sea of light?
Or since those drops are all sent back
So sure to thee, that none doth lack,
Why should frail flesh doubt any more
That what God takes, hee'l not restore?
O useful Element and clear!
My sacred wash and cleanser here,
My first consigner unto those
Fountains of life, where the Lamb goes?
What sublime truths, and wholesome themes,
Lodge in thy mystical, deep streams!
Such as dull man can never find
Unless that Spirit lead his mind,
Which first upon thy face did move,
And hatch'd all with his quick'ning love.
As this loud brook's incessant fall
In streaming rings restagnates all,
Which reach by course the bank, and then
Are no more seen, just so pass men.
O my invisible estate,
My glorious liberty, still late!
Thou art the Channel my soul seeks,
Not this with Cataracts and Creeks.

John Bunyan (1628–1688)

The Pilgrim

Who would true valor see
   Let him come hither!
Once here will constant be,
   Come wind, come weather:
There's no discouragement
Shall make him once relent
His first avow'd intent
   To be a Pilgrim.

Whoso beset him round
   With dismal stories,
Do but themselves confound;
   His strength the more is.
No lion can him fright;
He'll with a giant fight;
But he will have a right
   To be a Pilgrim.

Hobgoblin, nor foul fiend,
   Can daunt his spirit;
He knows he at the end
   Shall Life inherit—
Then, fancies, fly away;
He'll not fear what men say;
He'll labour, night and day,
   To be a Pilgrim.

Thomas Traherne (1636?–1674)

Poverty

As in the House I sat
Alone and desolate,
No Creature but the Fire and I,
The Chimney and the Stool, I lift mine Eye
Up to the Wall,
And in the silent Hall
Saw nothing mine
But some few Cups and Dishes shine
The Table and the wooden Stools
Where People us'd to dine:
A painted Cloth there was
Wherin some ancient Story wrought
A little entertain'd my Thought
Which Light discover'd through the Glass.

I wonder'd much to see
That all my Wealth should be
Confin'd in such a little Room,
Yet hope for more I scarcely durst presume.
It griev'd me fore
That such a scanty Store
Should be my All:
For I forgot my Ease and Health,
Nor did I think of Hands or Eyes,
Nor Soul nor Body prize;

I neither thought the Sun,
Nor Moon, nor Stars, nor People, *mine*,
Though they did round about me shine;
And therefore was I quite undone.

Some greater things I thought
Must needs for me be wrought,
Which till my craving Mind could see
I ever should lament my Poverty:
I fain would have
Whatever Bounty gave;
Nor could there be
Without, or Love or Deity:
For, should not He be Infinite
Whose Hand created me?
Ten thousand absent things
Did vex my poor and wanting Mind,
Which, till I be no longer blind,
Let me not see the King of Kings.

His Love must surely be
Rich, infinite, and free;
Nor can He be thought a God
Of Grace and Pow'r, that fills not his Abode,
His Holy Court,
In kind and liberal Sort;
Joys and Pleasures,
Plenty of Jewels, Goods, and Treasures
(To enrich the Poor, cheer the forlorn),
His Palace must adorn,

And given all to me:
For till *His* Works *my* Wealth became,
No Love, or Peace, did me enflame:
But now I have a Deity.

Insatiableness

I
No Walls confine! Can nothing hold my Mind?
Can I no Rest nor Satisfaction find?
     Must I behold Eternity
            And see
    What Things above the Heav'ns be?
       Will nothing serve the Turn?
    Nor Earth, nor Seas, nor Skies?
      Till I what lies
   In Time's beginning find;
Must I till then for ever burn?

Not all the Crowns; not all the heaps of Gold
On Earth; not all the Tales that can be told,
  Will Satisfaction yield to me:
            Nor Tree,
  Nor Shade, nor Sun, nor *Eden*, be
    A Joy: Nor Gems in Gold
    (Be't Pearl or precious Stone),
      Nor Spring, nor Flowers,
   Answer my *Craving* Powers,
Nor any Thing that Eyes behold.

Till I what was before all Time descry,
The World's Beginning seems but Vanity.
   My Soul doth there long Thoughts extend;
               No End
   Doth find, or Being comprehend:
      Yet somewhat sees that is
      The obscure shady face
         Of endless Space,
   All Room within; where I
Expect to meet Eternal Bliss.

II

   This busy, vast, enquiring Soul
         Brooks no Control,
     No Limits will endure,
   Nor any Rest: It will all see,
Not Time alone, but ev'n Eternity.
        What is it? Endless sure.
  'Tis mean Ambition to desire
       A single World:
    To many I aspire,
Tho one upon another hurl'd:
Nor will they all, if they be all confin'd,
       Delight my Mind.

   This busy, vast, enquiring Soul
         Brooks no Control:
       'Tis very curious too.
   Each one of all those Worlds must be
Enricht with infinite Variety
       And Worth; or 'twill not do.

'Tis nor Delight nor perfect Pleasure
To have a Purse
That hath a Bottom in its Treasure,
Since I must thence endless Expence disburse.
Sure there's a GOD (for else there's no Delight)
One Infinite.

John Norris (1637–1711)

The Aspiration

How long, great God, how long must I
Immured in this dark prison lie!
Where at the gates and avenues of sense
My Soul must watch to have intelligence;
Where but faint gleams of thee salute my sight,
Like doubtful moonshine in a cloudy night.
When shall I leave this magic Sphere,
And be all mind, all eye, all ear.

How cold this clime! and yet my sense
Perceives even here thy influence.
Even here thy strong magnetic charms I feel,
And pant and tremble like the amorous steel.
To lower good, and beauties less divine,
Sometimes my erroneous needle does decline;
But yet so strong the sympathy,
It turns, and points again to thee.

I long to see this excellence
Which at such distance strikes my sense.
My impatient Soul struggles to disengage
Her wings from the confinement of her cage.
Would'st thou great Love this prisoner once set free,
How would she hasten to be link'd with thee!
   She'd for no angel's conduct stay,
   But fly, and love on all the way.

The Resignation

   Long have I view'd, long have I thought,
And held with trembling hand this bitter draught:
   'Twas now just to my lips applied;
Nature shrank in, and all my courage died.
   But now resolv'd and firm I'll be,
Since, Lord, 'tis mingled, and reach'd out by thee.

   Since 'tis thy sentence I should part
With the most precious treasure of my heart,
   I freely that and more resign;
My heart itself, as its delight, is thine;
   My little all I give to thee—
Thou gav'st a greater gift, thy Son, to me.

   He left true bliss and joys above,
Himself he emptied of all good, but love;
   For me he freely did forsake
More good than he from me can ever take.
   A mortal life for a divine
He took, and did at last even that resign.

Take all, great God, I will not grieve,
But still will wish that I had still to give.
    I hear thy voice; thou bid'st me quit
My paradise, I bless and do submit.
    I will not murmur at thy word,
Nor beg thy angel to sheath up his sword.

Anne Finch, Countess of Winchilsea (1661–1720)

Some Reflections: *In a dialogue between Teresa and Ardelia, on the second and third verses of the 73rd Psalm*

> *My feet were almost gone, my treadings had well nigh
> slipped; and why, I was grieved at the wicked, I did also
> see the ungodly in such prosperity.*

Teresa

Hither, Ardelia, I your steps pursue,
    No solitude shou'd e're exclude a friend,
Your griefs I see, and as to friendship due,
    Demand the cause, to which these sorrows tend,
    What their beginnings were, and what may be their end?

Ardelia

Alas! Ardelia is not vainly sad,
    Nor to the clouds, that shade my careful brow,
Can fancies, dark and false suggestions add,
    But my Teresa, since you wish to know,
    I all my cares will tell, and all my griefs will show.

How, I my God and his just laws adore,
    How I have serv'd him, with my early years,
How I have lov'd his Name, and fear'd his Pow'r,
    Witness his Temples, where my falling tears,
    Have follow'd still my faults, and usher'd in my fears.

But oh! this God, the Glorious Architect
    Of this fair world, of this large Globe we see,
Seems those who trust him most, most to neglect,
    Else my Teresa, else, how could it be,
That all his storms attend, and tempests fall on me.

The Proud he hates, yet me he does expose
    Empty of all things, naked to their scorn.
His world, on them he liberally bestows,
    Theirs are his Vines, his fields, his flocks, his corn,
    And all that can sustain, and all that can adorn.

These are the men possess the mighty store,
    Compass the Earth, and with the boundless Deep
All they bestow receive again, with more;
    Whilst I, in fears to lose, and cares to keep,
    Obtain but daily bread, with interrupted sleep.

Teresa

Ardelia, hold, if more thou hast to say
    On this pernicious subject, let it die;
The subtle Fiend that leads thy soul astray,
    Thou doest not in this hour of sin descry,
    Oh! if we wander once, how soon the serpent's nigh.

Art thou content, to have thy portion here,
 The Tyrian purple, and the costly fare,
The purchase waits thee, but will cost thee dear,
 For mighty sums of Vice, thou must not spare,
  Do, as the wicked does, and thou, with him may'st share?

Canst thou repine, that Earth is not thy lot,
 And in that want, thy bounteous God distrust,
Confining all his mercies to that spot?
 Others of weight, acknowledge sure, we must,
  Or be to truth oppos'd, and Providence unjust.

Who seals thy forehead when the Plague is nigh,
 Ere the destroying Angel can descend?
Who guides th' avenging shafts that o're thee fly?
 When thou didst yet upon the breast depend,
  Who was thy Father then, and who was then thy friend?

Who gave his blood, when thine could not suffice
 To pay thy debt, who for thee sigh'd and wept,
And bought that Glory, at a wondrous price,
 Which is to future Ages for thee kept,
  Unless thou choose this world, and that to come, neglect?

Who leads thee through this Vale of tears below,
 To bring thee to thy Country, safe at last?
Who in the way does all thou want'st below,
 For more than this, his sacred word n'ere passed,
  And all thou truly want'st, assuredly thou hast?

What if to prove thee, when the billows rise,
    He from thy danger turns, and seems to sleep,
Wilt thou to murmurs straight convert thy cries,
    The crowd we see, the shore may safely keep,
    Whilst the distinguish'd twelve are threatn'd by the deep?

Ardelia

Teresa, from my guilty dream I wake,
    The truth has reach'd me, and my fault I find,
Forgive me, God, forgive the short mistake,
    How cou'd it enter my deluded mind,
That all both Worlds cou'd give was for one Wretch design'd?

I saw the Mighty, and began to slide,
    My feet were gone, but I return again,
And would not with them here the spoils divide;
    Nor look'd I at the end of Glorious men,
    Nor thought how lost they were, nor how abandon'd then.

A while, the Servant of Elisha so,
    Although his Master's pow'r with Heav'n he knew,
His faith forgoes, surrounded with the foe,
    Till by the Prophet's pray'r, the Vail withdrew
    And show'd the doubted aid of Providence in view.

Thomas Shepherd (1665–1739) and
John Mason (d. 1694)

For Communion with God

I

Alas, my God, that we should be
   Such Strangers to each other!
O that as Friends we might agree,
   And walk and talk together!
Thou know'st, my Soul does dearly love
   The Place of thine Abode;
No Music drops so sweet a Sound,
   As these two Words, MY GOD.

II

I long not for the Fruit that grows
   Within these Gardens here;
I find no sweetness in their Rose
   When Jesus is not near:
Thy gracious Presence, O my Christ,
   Can make a Paradise;
Ah, what are all the goodly Pearls
   Unto this Pearl of Price.

III

May I taste that Communion, Lord,
   Thy People have with thee?
Thy Spirit daily talks with them,
   O let it talk with me:

Like ENOCH, let me walk with God,
    And thus walk out my Day,
Attended with the Heav'nly Guards,
    Upon the King's High-way.

IV

When wilt thou come unto me, Lord?
    O come, my Lord most dear;
Come near, come nearer, nearer still;
    I'm well when thou art near.
When wilt thou come unto me, Lord?
    I languish for thy Sight;
Ten Thousand Suns, if thou art strange,
    Are Shades instead of Light.

V

When wilt thou come unto me, Lord?
    For till thou dost appear,
I count each Moment for a Day,
    Each Minute for a Year:
Come, Lord, and never from me go,
    This World's a darksome Place;
I find no Pleasure here below,
    When thou dost veil thy Face.

VI

There's no such Thing as Pleasure here,
    My Jesus is my all;
As thou dost thine, or disappear,
    My Pleasures rise and fall:

Come spread thy Savour on my Frame,
   No Sweetness is so sweet;
'Till I get up to sing thy Name,
   Where all thy Singers meet.

ᚻᚻᚻ

John Mason (d. 1694)

A Song of Praise for the Morning

My God was with me all this night,
   And gave me sweet repose:
My God did watch, even whilst I slept,
   Or I had never rose.
How many groan'd and wish'd for sleep,
   Until they wish'd for day,
Measuring slow hours with their quick pains,
   Whilst I securely lay!

Whilst I did sleep all dangers slept,
   No thieves did me affright;
Those ev'ning wolves, those beasts of prey,
   Disturbers of the night.
No raging flames nor storms did rend
   The house that I was in;
I heard no dreadful cries without,
   No doleful groans within.

What terrors have I scap'd this night,
   Which have on others fell!

My body might have slept its last;
    My soul have wak'd in hell.
Sweet rest hath gain'd that strength to me,
    Which labor did devour:
My body was in weakness sown,
    But it is rais'd in power.

Lord, for the mercies of the night,
    My humble thanks I pay;
And unto thee I dedicate
    The first-fruits of the day.
Let this day praise thee, O my God,
    And so let all my days:
And, O let mine eternal day
    Be thine eternal praise.

A Song of Praise for Grace

O God of grace, who hast restor'd
    Thine image unto me,
Which by my sins was quite defac'd,
    What shall I render thee!
Thine image and inscription, Lord,
    Upon my heart I bear:
Thine own I render unto thee,
    O God, my God most dear.

Myself I owe thee for myself,
    Whom thou didst make of earth;
But thou hast made me o'er again,
    Thou gav'st a second birth.

Twice born, and twice endu'd with life,
    I haste to come to thee,
To pay my vows, my thanks, my heart,
    With all humility.

O, was I born first from beneath,
    And then born from above!
Am I a child of man and God?
    O rich and endless love!
When I had broke the tables, Lord,
    New tables thou didst hew;
And with thy finger didst engrave
    Thy laws on them anew.

Earth is my mother, earth my nurse,
    And earth must be my tomb:
Yet God, the God of heaven and earth,
    My Father is become.
Hell enter'd me, and into hell
    I quickly should have run;
But, O! kind heav'n laid hold on me:
    Heav'n is in me begun.

This spark will rise into a flame,
    This seed into a tree;
My songs shall rise, my praises shall
    Loud hallelujahs be.

Charles Wesley (1707–1788)

"Gentle Jesus, meek and mild"

1 Gentle Jesus, meek and mild,
   Look upon a little child;
   Pity my simplicity,
   Suffer me to come to Thee.

2 Fain I would to Thee be brought;
   Dearest God, forbid it not;
   Give me, dearest God, a place
   In the kingdom of Thy grace.

3 Put Thy hands upon my head;
   Let me in Thine arms be stay'd;
   Let me lean upon Thy breast;
   Lull me, lull me, Lord, to rest.

4 Hold me fast in Thine embrace,
   Let me see Thy smiling face;
   Give me, Lord, Thy blessing give;
   Pray for me, and I shall live:

5 I shall live the simple life,
   Free from sin's uneasy strife;
   Sweetly ignorant of ill,
   Innocent and happy still.

6 O that I may never know
   What the wicked people do!
   Sin is contrary to Thee,
   Sin is the forbidden tree.

7 Keep me from the great offence,
   Guard my helpless innocence;
   Hide me, from all evil hide,
   Self, and stubbornness, and pride.

⚬

Christopher Smart (1722–1771)

Faith

I

The Father of the Faithful said,
   At God's first calling, "Here am I";
Let us by his example sway'd,
   Like him submit, like him reply.

II

"Go take thy son, thine only son,
   "And offer him to God thy King."
The word was giv'n: the work begun,
   "The altar pile, the victim bring."

III

But lo! th' angelic voice above
   Bade the great Patriarch stop his hands;

"Know God is everlasting love,
    "And must revoke such harsh commands."

IV

Then let us imitate the Seer,
    And tender with compliant grace
Ourselves, our souls, and children here,
    Hereafter in a better place.

Taste

I

O Guide my judgment and my taste,
    Sweet Spirit, author of the book
Of wonders, told in language chaste
    And plainness, not to be mistook.

II

O let me muse, and yet at sight
    The page admire, the page believe;
"Let there be light, and there was light,
    "Let there be Paradise and Eve!"

III

Who his foul's rapture can refrain?
    At Joseph's ever-pleasing tale,
Of marvels, the prodigious train,
    To Sinai's hill from Goshen's vale.

IV

The Psalmist and proverbial Seer,
    And all the prophet's sons of song,
Make all things precious, all things dear,
    And bear the brilliant word along.

V

O take the book from off the shelf,
    And con it meekly on thy knees;
Best panegyric on itself,
    And self-avouch'd to teach and please.

VI

Respect, adore it heart and mind.
    How greatly sweet, how sweetly grand,
Who reads the most, is most refin'd,
    And polish'd by the Master's hand.

Hymn to the Supreme Being

On Recovery from a Dangerous Fit of Illness

When Israel's ruler on the royal bed
    In anguish and in perturbation lay,
The down relieved not his anointed head,
    And rest gave place to horror and dismay.
Fast flow'd the tears, high heaved each gasping sigh,
When God's own Prophet thunder'd, "Monarch, thou must
    die!"

And must I go, the illustrious mourner cry'd,
    I who have serv'd thee still in faith and truth,
Whose snow white conscience no foul crime has dy'd
    From youth to manhood, infancy to youth,
Like David, who have still revered thy word,
The sovereign of myself and servant of the Lord.

The Judge Almighty heard his suppliant's moan,
    Repeal'd his sentence, and his health restored;
The beams of mercy on his temples shone,
    Shot from that heaven to which his sigh's had soar'd;
The sun retreated at his Maker's nod,
And miracles confirm the genuine work of God.

But, O immortals! what had I to plead
When death stood o'er me with his threat'ning lance,
When reason left me in the time of need,
    And sense was left in terror or in trance,
My sinking soul was with my blood inflamed,
    And the celestial image sunk, defac'd, and maim'd.

I sent back memory in heedful guise,
    To search the records of preceding years;
Home, like the raven to the ark, she flies,
    Croaking bad tidings to my trembling ears.
O sun, again, that thy retreat was made,
And threw my follies back into the friendly shade!

But who are they that bid affliction cease!—
    Redemption and forgiveness, heavenly sounds!
Behold the dove that brings the branch of peace,
    Behold the balm that heals the gaping wounds—
Vengeance divine's by penitence supprest—
She struggles with the angel, conquers, and is blest.

Yet hold, presumption, nor too fondly climb,
    And thou too hold, O horrible despair!
In man humility's alone sublime,
    Who diffidently hopes he's Christ's own care—
O all sufficient Lamb! in death's dread hour
Thy merits who shall slight, or who can doubt thy power?

But soul-rejoicing health again returns,
    The blood meanders gentle in each vein,
The lamp of life renew'd with vigor burns,
    And exiled reason takes her seat again—
Brisk leaps the heart, the mind's at large once more,
To love, to praise, to bless, to wonder and adore.

The virtuous partner of my nuptial bands,
    Appear'd a widow to my frantic sight;
My little prattlers lifting up their hands,
    Beckon me back to them, to life, and light;
I come, ye spotless sweets! I come again,
Nor have your tears been shed, nor have ye knelt in vain.

All glory to the Eternal, to the Immense,
    All glory to the Omniscient and Good,
Whose power's uncircumscribed, whose love's intense;
    But yet whose justice ne'er could be withstood.
Except through him—through him, who stands alone,
Of worth, of weight, allow'd for all mankind to atone!

He raised the lame, the lepers he made whole,
    He fix'd the palsied nerves of weak decay,
He drove out Satan from the tortured soul,
    And to the blind, gave or restored the day—
Nay more . . . far more unequall'd pangs sustain'd,
Till his last fallen flock his taintless blood regain'd.

My feeble feet refused my body's weight,
    Nor would my eyes admit the glorious light,
My nerves convulsed, shook, fearful of their fate,
    My mind lay open to the powers of night.
He, pitying, did a second birth bestow
A birth of joy—not like the first of tears and woe.

Ye strengthen'd feet, forth to his altar move;
    Quicken, ye new-strung nerves, the enraptured lyre;
Ye heav'n-directed eyes, o'erflow with love;
    Glow, glow, my soul, with pure seraphic fire;
Deeds, thoughts, and words, no more his mandates break,
But to his endless glory work, conceive, and speak.

O! penitence, to virtue near allied,
    Thou canst new joys e'en to the blest impart:
The listening angels lay their harps aside
    To hear the music of the contrite heart;
And heaven itself wears a more radiant face,
When charity presents thee to the throne of grace,

Chief of metallic forms is regal gold;
    Of elements, the limpid fount that flows;
Give me 'mongst gems the brilliant to behold;
    O'er Flora's flock imperial is the rose;
Above all birds the sovereign eagle soars;
And monarch of the field the lordly lion roars.

What can with great leviathan compare,
    Who takes his pastime in the mighty main?
What, like the sun, shines through the realms of air,
    And gilds and glorifies the ethereal plain...
Yet what are these to man, who bears the sway;
For all was made for him—to serve, and to obey.

Thus in high heaven Charity is great,
    Faith, Hope, Devotion, hold a lower place;
On her the cherubs and the seraphs wait,
    Her, every virtue courts, and every grace;
See! on the right, close by the Almighty's throne.
In him she shines confest, who came to make her known.

Deep-rooted in my heart then let her grow,
   That for the past the future may atone;
That I may act what thou hast given to know,
   That I may live for thee, and thee alone,
And justify those sweetest words from heaven,
"That he shall love thee most to whom thou'st most forgiven."

John Newton (1725–1807)

The Name of Jesus

How sweet the name of Jesus sounds
   In a believer's ear!
It soothes his sorrows, heals his wounds,
   And drives away his fear.

It makes the wounded spirit whole,
   And calms the troubled breast;
'Tis manna to the hungry soul,
   And to the weary rest.

Dear name! the rock on which I build,
   My shield and hiding-place;
My never-failing treas'ry, fill'd
   With boundless stores of grace.

By thee my prayers' acceptance gain,
  Although with sin defil'd;
Satan accuses me in vain,
  And I am own'd a child.

Jesus! my Shepherd, Husband, Friend,
  My Prophet, Priest, and King;
My Lord, my Life, my Way, my End,
  Accept the praise I bring.

Weak is the effort of my heart,
  And cold my warmest thought;
But when I see thee as thou art,
  I'll praise thee as I ought.

Till then I would thy love proclaim
  With ev'ry fleeting breath;
And may the music of thy name
  Refresh my soul in death.

Looking at the Cross

In evil long I took delight,
  Unaw'd by shame or fear,
Till a new object struck my sight,
  And stopp'd my wild career.

I saw one hanging on a tree,
   In agonies and blood,
Who fix'd his languid eyes on me,
   As near his cross I stood.

Sure never till my latest breath,
   Can I forget that look;
It seemed to charge me with his death,
   Though not a word he spoke.

My conscience felt, and own'd the guilt,
   And plunged me in despair;
I saw my sins his blood had spilt,
   And help'd to nail him there.

Alas! I knew not what I did;
   But now my tears are vain;
Where shall my trembling soul be hid?
   For I the Lord have slain.

A second look he gave, which said,
   "I freely all forgive;
This blood is for thy ransom paid,
   I die, that thou may'st live."

Thus, while his death my sin displays
   In all its blackest hue
(Such is the mystery of grace),
   It seals my pardon too.

With pleasing grief and mournful joy
   My spirit now is fill'd,
That I should such a life destroy,
   Yet live by him I kill'd.

∽

William Cowper (1731–1800)

Walking with God

Gen. v. 24
Oh for a closer walk with God!
   A calm and heavenly frame;
A light to shine upon the road
   That leads me to the Lamb!

Where is the blessedness I knew
   When first I saw the Lord?
Where is the soul-refreshing view
   Of Jesus and his word?

What peaceful hours I once enjoyed!
   How sweet their memory still!
But they have left an aching void
   The world can never fill.

Return, O holy Dove, return,
   Sweet messenger of rest!
I hate the sins that made thee mourn,
   And drove thee from my breast.

The dearest idol I have known,
    Whate'er that idol be,
Help me to tear it from thy throne,
    And worship only thee.

So shall my walk be close with God,
    Calm and serene my frame;
So purer light shall mark the road
    That leads me to the Lamb.

Jehovah-Rophi

I AM THE LORD THAT HEALETH THEE

Exod. xv. 26

Heal us, Emmanuel! here we are,
    Waiting to feel thy touch:
Deep-wounded souls to thee repair,
    And, Saviour, we are such.

Our faith is feeble, we confess,
    We faintly trust thy word;
But wilt thou pity us the less?
    Be that far from thee, Lord!

Remember him who once applied,
    With trembling, for relief;
"Lord, I believe," with tears he cried,
    "Oh, help my unbelief!"

She too, who touched thee in the press,
  And healing virtue stole,
Was answered, "Daughter, go in peace,
  Thy faith hath made thee whole."

Concealed amid the gathering throng,
  She would have shunned thy view;
And if her faith was firm and strong,
  Had strong misgivings too.

Like her, with hopes and fears we come,
  To touch thee, if we may;
Oh! send us not despairing home!
  Send none unhealed away!

The Contrite Heart

Isaiah lvii. 15
The Lord will happiness divine
  On contrite hearts bestow;
Then tell me, gracious God, is mine
  A contrite heart, or no?

I hear, but seem to hear in vain,
  Insensible as steel;
If aught is felt, 'tis only pain,
  To find I cannot feel.

I sometimes think myself inclined
    To love thee, if I could;
But often feel another mind,
    Averse to all that's good.

My best desires are faint and few,
    I fain would strive for more;
But when I cry, "My strength renew!"
    Seem weaker than before.

Thy saints are comforted, I know,
    And love thy house of prayer;
I therefore go where others go,
    But find no comfort there.

Oh make this heart rejoice or ache;
    Decide this doubt for me;
And if it be not broken, break,—
    And heal it if it be.

Ephraim Repenting

Jer. xxxi. 18–20
My God, till I received thy stroke,
    How like a beast was I!
So unaccustomed to the yoke,
    So backward to comply.

With grief my just reproach I bear;
    Shame fills me at the thought,
How frequent my rebellions were,
    What wickedness I wrought.

Thy merciful restraint I scorned,
    And left the pleasant road;
Yet turn me, and I shall be turned!
    Thou art the Lord my God.

"Is Ephraim banished from my thoughts,
    Or vile in my esteem?
"No," saith the Lord, "with all his faults,
    I still remember him."

"Is he a dear and pleasant child?"
    "Yes, dear and pleasant still;
Though sin his foolish heart beguiled,
    And he withstood my will.

"My sharp rebuke has laid him low,
    He seeks my face again;
My pity kindles at his woe,
    He shall not seek in vain."

Peace After a Storm

When darkness long has veiled my mind,
    And smiling day once more appears,
Then, my Redeemer, then I find
    The folly of my doubts and fears.

Straight I upbraid my wandering heart,
    And blush that I should ever be
Thus prone to act so base a part,
    Or harbor one hard thought of thee.

Oh! let me then at length be taught
    What I am still so slow to learn;
That God is Love, and changes not,
    Nor knows the shadow of a turn.

Sweet truth, and easy to repeat!
    But when my faith is sharply tried,
I find myself a learner yet,
    Unskilful, weak, and apt to slide.

But, O my Lord, one look from thee
    Subdues the disobedient will,
Drives doubt and discontent away,
    And thy rebellious worm is still.

Thou art as ready to forgive
    As I am ready to repine;
Thou, therefore, all the praise receive;
    Be shame and self-abhorrence mine.

Joy and Peace in Believing

Sometimes a light surprises
    The Christian while he sings;
It is the Lord who rises
    With healing in his wings:
When comforts are declining,
    He grants the soul again
A season of clear shining,
    To cheer it after rain.

In holy contemplation,
    We sweetly then pursue
The theme of God's salvation,
    And find it ever new:
Set free from present sorrow,
    We cheerfully can say,
E'en let the unknown to-morrow
    Bring with it what it may!

It can bring with it nothing
    But he will bear us through;
Who gives the lilies clothing
    Will clothe his people too;
Beneath the spreading heavens
    No creature but is fed;
And he who feeds the ravens
    Will give his children bread.

Though vine nor fig-tree neither
   Their wonted fruit shall bear,
Though all the field should wither,
   Nor flocks nor herds be there:
Yet God the same abiding,
   His praise shall tune my voice;
      For, while in him confiding,
      I cannot but rejoice.

∾

Augustus Toplady (1740–1778)

A Prayer: Living and Dying

Rock of ages, cleft for me,
Let me hide myself in Thee!
Let the Water and the Blood,
From thy riven Side which flow'd,
Be of sin the double cure;
Cleanse me from its guilt and pow'r.

Not the labors of my hands
Can fulfil thy law's demands;
Could my zeal no respite know,
Could my tears for ever flow,
All for sin could not atone:
Thou must save, and Thou alone.

Nothing in my hand I bring;
Simply to thy Cross I cling;
Naked, come to Thee for dress;
Helpless, look to Thee for grace;
Foul, I to the Fountain fly;
Wash me, Saviour, or I die!

While I draw this fleeting breath—
When my eyestrings break in death—
When I soar through tracts unknown—
See Thee on Thy Judgement-throne—
ROCK of ages, cleft for me,
Let me hide myself in Thee!

William Blake (1757–1827)

"Mock on, Mock on, Voltaire, Rousseau"

Mock on, Mock on, Voltaire, Rousseau,
Mock on, Mock on! tis all in vain!
You throw the sand against the wind
And the wind blows it back again

And every sand becomes a Gem
Reflected in the beams divine
Blown back they blind the mocking Eye
But still in Israel's paths they shine

The Atoms of Democritus
And Newton's Particles of light
Are sands upon the Red Sea shore
Where Israel's tents do shine so bright

The Little Boy Lost

"Father! father! where are you going?
O do not walk so fast.
Speak, father, speak to your little boy,
Or else I shall be lost."

The night was dark, no father was there;
The child was wet with dew;
The mire was deep, & the child did weep,
And away the vapour flew.

∾

William Wordsworth (1770–1850)

"Not seldom, clad in radiant vest"

Not seldom, clad in radiant vest,
Deceitfully goes forth the morn;
Not seldom evening in the west
Sinks smilingly forsworn.

The smoothest seas will sometimes prove,
To the confiding bark, untrue;
And, if she trust the stars above
They can be treacherous too.

The umbrageous oak, in pomp outspread,
Full oft, when storms the welkin rend,
Draws lightning down upon the head
It promised to defend.

But thou art true, incarnate Lord,
Who didst vouchsafe for man to die;
Thy smile is sure, thy plighted word
No change can falsify!

I bent before thy gracious throne,
And asked for peace on suppliant knee;
And peace was given,—not peace alone,
But faith sublimed to ecstasy!

Resolution and Independence

I

There was a roaring in the wind all night;
The rain came heavily and fell in floods;
But now the sun is rising calm and bright;
The birds are singing in the distant woods;
Over his own sweet voice the Stock-dove broods;
The Jay makes answer as the Magpie chatters;
And all the air is filled with pleasant noise of waters.

II

All things that love the sun are out of doors;
The sky rejoices in the morning's birth;
The grass is bright with rain-drops—on the moors
The hare is running races in her mirth;
And with her feet she from the plashy earth
Raises a mist, that, glittering in the sun,
Runs with her all the way, wherever she doth run.

III

I was a Traveller then upon the moor,
I saw the hare that raced about with joy;
I heard the woods and distant waters roar;
Or heard them not, as happy as a boy:
The pleasant season did my heart employ:
My old remembrances went from me wholly;
And all the ways of men, so vain and melancholy.

IV

But, as it sometimes chanceth, from the might
Of joy in minds that can no further go,
As high as we have mounted in delight
In our dejection do we sink as low;
To me that morning did it happen so;
And fears and fancies thick upon me came;
Dim sadness—and blind thoughts, I knew not, nor could name.

V

I heard the sky-lark warbling in the sky;
And I bethought me of the playful hare:

Even such a happy Child of earth am I;
Even as these blissful creatures do I fare;
Far from the world I walk, and from all care;
But there may come another day to me—
Solitude, pain of heart, distress, and poverty.

VI

My whole life I have lived in pleasant thought,
As if life's business were a summer mood;
As if all needful things would come unsought
To genial faith, still rich in genial good;
But how can He expect that others should
Build for him, sow for him, and at his call
Love him, who for himself will take no heed at all?

VII

I thought of Chatterton, the marvellous Boy,
The sleepless Soul that perished in his pride;
Of Him who walked in glory and in joy
Following his plough, along the mountain-side:
By our own spirits are we deified:
We Poets in our youth begin in gladness;
But thereof come in the end despondency and madness.

VIII

Now, whether it were by peculiar grace,
A leading from above, a something given,
Yet it befell, that, in this lonely place,
When I with these untoward thoughts had striven,
Beside a pool bare to the eye of heaven
I saw a Man before me unawares:
The oldest man he seemed that ever wore grey hairs.

IX

As a huge stone is sometimes seen to lie
Couched on the bald top of an eminence;
Wonder to all who do the same espy,
By what means it could thither come, and whence;
So that it seems a thing endued with sense:
Like a sea-beast crawled forth, that on a shelf
Of rock or sand reposeth, there to sun itself;

X

Such seemed this Man, not all alive nor dead,
Nor all asleep—in his extreme old age:
His body was bent double, feet and head
Coming together in life's pilgrimage;
As if some dire constraint of pain, or rage
Of sickness felt by him in times long past,
A more than human weight upon his frame had cast.

XI

Himself he propped, limbs, body, and pale face,
Upon a long grey staff of shaven wood:
And, still as I drew near with gentle pace,
Upon the margin of that moorish flood
Motionless as a cloud the old Man stood,
That heareth not the loud winds when they call
And moveth all together, if it move at all.

XII

At length, himself unsettling, he the pond
Stirred with his staff, and fixedly did look

Upon the muddy water, which he conned,
As if he had been reading in a book:
And now a stranger's privilege I took;
And, drawing to his side, to him did say,
"This morning gives us promise of a glorious day."

XIII

A gentle answer did the old Man make,
In courteous speech which forth he slowly drew:
And him with further words I thus bespake,
"What occupation do you there pursue?
This is a lonesome place for one like you."
Ere he replied, a flash of mild surprise
Broke from the sable orbs of his yet-vivid eyes,

XIV

His words came feebly, from a feeble chest,
But each in solemn order followed each,
With something of a lofty utterance drest—
Choice word and measured phrase, above the reach
Of ordinary men; a stately speech;
Such as grave Livers do in Scotland use,
Religious men, who give to God and man their dues.

XV

He told, that to these waters he had come
To gather leeches, being old and poor:
Employment hazardous and wearisome!
And he had many hardships to endure:
From pond to pond he roamed, from moor to moor;

Housing, with God's good help, by choice or chance,
And in this way he gained an honest maintenance.

XVI

The old Man still stood talking by my side;
But now his voice to me was like a stream
Scarce heard; nor word from word could I divide;
And the whole body of the Man did seem
Like one whom I had met with in a dream;
Or like a man from some far region sent,
To give me human strength, by apt admonishment.

XVII

My former thoughts returned; the fear that kills;
And hope that is unwilling to be fed;
Cold, pain, and labour, and all fleshly ills;
And mighty Poets in their misery dead.
—Perplexed, and longing to be comforted,
My question eagerly did I renew,
"How is it that you live, and what is it you do?"

XVIII

He with a smile did then his words repeat;
And said, that, gathering leeches, far and wide
He travelled; stirring thus above his feet
The waters of the pools where they abide.
"Once I could meet with them on every side;
But they have dwindled long by slow decay;
Yet still I persevere, and find them where I may."

XIX

While he was talking thus, the lonely place,
The old Man's shape, and speech—all troubled me:
In my mind's eye I seemed to see him pace
About the weary moors continually,
Wandering about alone and silently.
While I these thoughts within myself pursued,
He, having made a pause, the same discourse renewed.

XX

And soon with this he other matter blended,
Cheerfully uttered, with demeanour kind,
But stately in the main; and when he ended,
I could have laughed myself to scorn to find
In that decrepit Man so firm a mind.
"God," said I, "be my help and stay secure;
I'll think of the Leech-gatherer on the lonely moor!"

✑

John Clare (1793–1864)

The Poet's Swan-Song

I am! yet what I am who cares, or knows?
    My friends forsake me like a memory lost.
I am the self-consumer of my woes,
    They rise and vanish, an oblivious host,
Shadows of life, whose very soul is lost.
    And yet I am—I live—though I am toss'd

Into the nothingness of scorn and noise,
    Into the living sea of waking dream,
Where there is neither sense of life, nor joys,
    But the huge shipwreck of my own esteem
And all that's dear. Even those I loved the best
    Are strange—nay, they are stranger than the rest.

I long for scenes where man has never trod,
    For scenes where woman never smiled or wept;
There to abide with my Creator, God,
    And sleep as I in childhood sweetly slept
Full of high thoughts, unborn. So let me lie,
The grass below; above the vaulted sky.

John Henry Newman (1801–1890)

The Pillar of the Cloud

Lead, Kindly Light, amid the encircling gloom,
        Lead Thou me on!
The night is dark, and I am far from home—
        Lead Thou me on!
Keep Thou my feet; I do not ask to see
The distant scene—one step enough for me.

I was not ever thus, nor pray'd that Thou
        Shouldst lead me on.

I loved to choose and see my path, but now
      Lead Thou me on!
I loved the garish day, and, spite of fears,
Pride ruled my will: remember not past years.

So long Thy power hath blest me, sure it still
      Will lead me on,
O'er moor and fen, o'er crag and torrent, till
      The night is gone;
And with the morn those angel faces smile
Which I have loved long since, and lost awhile.

∼∕∕⌒

James Clarence Mangan (1803–1849)

St. Patrick's Hymn

May Christ, I pray,
Protect me to-day
      Against poison and fire,
Against drowning and wounding,
That so, in his grace abounding,
      I may earn the preacher's hire.

Christ, as a light,
Illumine and guide me!
Christ, as a shield, o'ershadow and cover me!
Christ be under me! Christ be over me!
      Christ be beside me
      On left hand and right!
Christ be before me, behind me, about me!

Christ this day be within and without me!
Christ, the lowly and the meek,
  Christ, the all-powerful, be
In the heart of each to whom I speak,
  In the mouth of each who speaks to me!
    In all who draw, near me,
    Or see me, or hear me!

Elizabeth Barrett Browning (1806–1861)

Comfort

Speak low to me, my Savior, low and sweet
From out the hallelujahs, sweet and low,
Lest I should fear and fall, and miss thee so,
Who art not missed by any that entreat.
Speak to me as to Mary at thy feet!
And if no precious gums my hands bestow,
Let my tears drop like amber, while I go
In reach of thy divinest voice complete
In humanest affection—thus, in sooth,
To lose the sense of losing. As a child,
Whose song-bird seeks the wood for evermore,
Is sung to in its stead by mother's mouth,
Till, sinking on her breast, love-reconciled,
He sleeps the faster that he wept before.

Alfred, Lord Tennyson (1809–1892)

In Memoriam A. H. H.
OBIIT MDCCCXXXIII

Strong Son of God, immortal Love,
 Whom we, that have not seen thy face,
 By faith, and faith alone, embrace,
Believing where we cannot prove;

Thine are these orbs of light and shade;
 Thou madest Life in man and brute;
 Thou madest Death; and lo, thy foot
Is on the skull which thou hast made.

Thou wilt not leave us in the dust;
 Thou madest man, he knows not why;
 He thinks he was not made to die;
And thou hast made him: thou art just.

Thou seemest human and divine,
 The highest, holiest manhood, thou:
 Our wills are ours, we know not how
Our wills are ours, to make them thine.

Our little systems have their day;
 They have their day and cease to be:
 They are but broken lights of thee,
And thou, O Lord, art more than they.

We have but faith: we cannot know;
    For knowledge is of things we see;
    And yet we trust it comes from thee,
A beam in darkness: let it grow.

Let knowledge grow from more to more,
    But more of reverence in us dwell;
    That mind and soul, according well,
May make one music as before,

But vaster. We are fools and slight;
    We mock thee when we do not fear:
    But help thy foolish ones to bear;
Help thy vain worlds to bear thy light.

Forgive what seem'd my sin in me;
    What seem'd my worth since I began;
    For merit lives from man to man,
And not from man, O Lord, to thee.

Forgive my grief for one removed,
    Thy creature, whom I found so fair.
    I trust he lives in thee, and there
I find him worthier to be loved.

Forgive these wild and wandering cries,
    Confusions of a wasted youth;
    Forgive them where they fail in truth,
And in thy wisdom make me wise.

Emily Brontë (1818–1848)

Last Lines

No coward soul is mine,
No trembler in the world's storm-troubled sphere:
I see Heaven's glories shine,
And faith shines equal, arming me from fear.

O God within my breast,
Almighty, ever-present Deity!
Life—that in me has rest,
As I—undying life—have power in thee!

Vain are the thousand creeds
That move men's hearts: unutterably vain;
Worthless as withered weeds,
Or idlest froth amid the boundless main,

To waken doubt in one
Holding so fast by thine infinity;
So surely anchored on
The steadfast rock of immortality.

With wide-embracing love
Thy spirit animates eternal years,
Pervades and broods above,
Changes, sustains, dissolves, creates, and rears.

Though earth and man were gone,
And suns and universes ceased to be,
And thou wert left alone,
Every existence would exist in thee.

There is not room for Death
Nor atom that his might could render void:
Thou—THOU art Being and Breath,
And what THOU art may never be destroyed.

Julia Ward Howe (1819–1910)

Battle-Hymn of the Republic

Mine eyes have seen the glory of the coming of the Lord:
He is trampling out the vintage where the grapes of wrath
 are stored;
He hath loosed the fateful lightning of his terrible swift
 sword:
    His truth is marching on.

I have seen Him in the watch-fires of a hundred circling camps;
They have builded Him an altar in the evening dews and
 damps;
I can read His righteous sentence by the dim and flaring lamps.
    His day is marching on.

I have read a fiery gospel, writ in burnished rows of steel:
"As ye deal with my contemners, so with you my grace shall
    deal;
Let the Hero, born of woman, crush the serpent with his heel,
        Since God is marching on."

He has sounded forth the trumpet that shall never call retreat;
He is sifting out the hearts of men before his judgment-seat:
Oh! be swift, my soul, to answer Him! be jubilant, my feet!
        Our God is marching on.

In the beauty of the lilies Christ was born across the sea,
With a glory in his bosom that transfigures you and me:
As he died to make men holy, let us die to make men free,
        While God is marching on.

∿

Josiah Gilbert Holland (1819–1881)

A Song of Doubt

The day is quenched, and the sun is fled;
    God has forgotten the world!
The moon is gone, and the stars are dead;
    God has forgotten the world!

Evil has won in the horrid feud
    Of ages with The Throne;
Evil stands on the neck of Good,
    And rules the world alone.

There is no good; there is no God;
   And Faith is a heartless cheat
Who bares the back for the Devil's rod,
   And scatters thorns for the feet.

What are prayers in the lips of death,
   Filling and chilling with hail?
What are prayers but wasted breath
   Beaten back by the gale?

The day is quenched, and the sun is fled;
   God has forgotten the world!
The moon is gone, and the stars are dead;
   God has forgotten the world!

A Song of Faith

Day will return with a fresher boon;
   God will remember the world!
Night will come with a newer moon;
   God will remember the world!

Evil is only the slave of Good;
   Sorrow the servant of Joy;
And the soul is mad that refuses food
   Of the meanest in God's employ.

The fountain of joy is fed by tears,
   And love is lit by the breath of sighs;
The deepest griefs and the wildest fears
   Have holiest ministries.

Strong grows the oak in the sweeping storm;
   Safely the flower sleeps under the snow;
And the farmer's hearth is never warm
   Till the cold wind starts to blow.

Day will return with a fresher boon;
   God will remember the world!
Night will come with a newer moon;
   God will remember the world!

✺

Anne Brontë (1820–1849)

The Doubter's Prayer

Eternal Power, of earth and air!
   Unseen, yet seen in all around;
Remote, but dwelling everywhere;
   Though silent, heard in every sound;

If e'er Thine ear in mercy bent,
   When wretched mortals cried to Thee,
And if, indeed, Thy Son was sent,
   To save lost sinners such as me:

Then hear me now, while kneeling here,
   I lift to Thee my heart and eye,
And all my soul ascends in prayer,
   Oh, give me—give me Faith! I cry.

Without some glimmering in my heart,
   I could not raise this fervent prayer;
But, oh! a stronger light impart,
   And in Thy mercy fix it there.

While Faith is with me, I am blest;
   It turns my darkest night to day;
But while I clasp it to my breast,
   I often feel it slide away.

Then, cold and dark, my spirit sinks,
   To see my light of life depart;
And every fiend of Hell, methinks,
   Enjoys the anguish of my heart.

What shall I do, if all my love,
   My hopes, my toil, are cast away,
And if there be no God above,
   To hear and bless me when I pray?

If this be vain delusion all,
   If death be an eternal sleep,
And none can hear my secret call,
   Or see the silent tears I weep!

Oh, help me, God! For Thou alone
    Canst my distracted soul relieve;
Forsake it not, it is Thine own,
    Though weak, yet longing to believe.

Oh, drive these cruel doubts away;
    And make me know that Thou art God!
A faith, that shines by night and day,
    Will lighten every earthly load.

If I believe that Jesus died,
    And waking, rose to reign above;
Then surely Sorrow, Sin, and Pride
    Must yield to Peace, and Hope, and Love;

And all the blessèd words He said
    Will strength and holy joy impart:
A shield of safety o'er my head,
    A spring of comfort in my heart.

ᕫᕒ

Matthew Arnold (1822–1888)

East London

'Twas August, and the fierce sun overhead
Smote on the squalid streets of Bethnal Green,
And the pale weaver, through his windows seen
In Spitalfields, looked thrice dispirited.

I met a preacher there I knew, and said:
"Ill and o'erworked, how fare you in this scene?"
"Bravely!" said he; "for I of late have been
Much cheered with thoughts of Christ, *the living bread.*"

O human soul! as long as thou canst so
Set up a mark of everlasting light,
Above the howling senses' ebb and flow,

To cheer thee, and to right thee if thou roam,
Not with lost toil thou labourest through the night!
Thou mak'st the heaven thou hop'st indeed thy home.

Ednah Dow Cheney (1824–1904)

The Larger Prayer

At first I prayed for Light:
    Could I but see the way,
How gladly, swiftly would I walk
    To everlasting day!

And next I prayed for Strength:
    That I might tread the road
With firm unfaltering feet, and win
    The heaven's serene abode.

And then I asked for Faith:
   Could I but trust my God,
I'd live enfolded in his peace,
   Though foes were all abroad.

But now I pray for Love:
   Deep love to God and man,
A living love that will not fail,
   However dark his plan.

And Light and Strength and Faith
   Are opening everywhere!
God only waited for me till
   I prayed the larger prayer.

‿ﾟ

William Allingham (1824–1889)

Loss

Grieve not much for loss of wealth,
   Loss of friends, or loss of fame,
Loss of years, or loss of health;
   Answer, hast thou lost the shame
Whose early tremor once could flush
Thy cheek, and make thine eyes to gush,
And send thy spirit, sad and sore,
To kneel with face upon the floor,

Burden'd with consciousness of sin?
Art thou cold and hard within,—
Sometimes looking back surprised
On thy old mood, scarce recognized,
As on a picture of thy face
In blooming childhood's transient grace?
Then hast thou cause for grief; and most
In seldom missing what is lost.
With the loss of Yesterday,
   Thou hast lost To-day, To-morrow,—
All thou mightst have been. O pray
    (If pray thou canst) for poignant sorrow!

Christina Georgina Rossetti (1830–1894)

A Christmas Carol

In the bleak mid-winter
   Frosty wind made moan,
Earth stood hard as iron,
   Water like a stone;
Snow had fallen, snow on snow,
   Snow on snow,
In the bleak mid-winter
   Long ago.

Our God, Heaven cannot hold Him
   Nor earth sustain;

Heaven and earth shall flee away
   When He comes to reign:
In the bleak mid-winter
   A stable-place sufficed
The Lord God Almighty
   Jesus Christ.

Enough for Him, whom cherubim
   Worship night and day,
A breastful of milk
   And a mangerful of hay;
Enough for Him, whom angels
   Fall down before,
The ox and ass and camel
   Which adore.

Angels and archangels
   May have gathered there,
Cherubim and seraphim
   Thronged the air;
But only His mother
   In her maiden bliss
Worshipped the Beloved
   With a kiss.

What can I give Him.
   Poor as I am?
If I were a shepherd
   I would bring a lamb,

If I were a Wise Man
   I would do my part—
Yet what I can I give Him,
   Give my heart.

Wrestling

   Alas my Lord,
How should I wrestle all the livelong night
With Thee my God, my strength and my delight?

   How can it need
So agonized an effort and a strain
To make Thy face of mercy shine again?

   How can it need
Such wringing out of breathless prayer to move
Thee to Thy wonted love, when Thou art Love?

   Yet Abraham
So hung about Thine arm, outstretcht and bared,
That for ten righteous Sodom had been spared.

   Yet Jacob did
So hold Thee by the clenchèd hand of prayer
That he prevailed and Thou didst bless him there.

   Elias prayed,
And sealed the founts of heaven: he prayed again,
And lo Thy blessing fell in showers of rain.

Gulpt by the fish
And by the pit, lost Jonah made his moan,
And Thou forgavest, waiting to atone.

All Nineveh
Fasting and girt in sackcloth raised a cry,
Which moved Thee ere the day of grace went by.

Thy Church prayed on
And on for blessed Peter in his strait,
Till opened of its own accord the gate.

Yea Thou my God
Hast prayed all night, and in the garden prayed,
Even while like melting wax Thy strength was made.

Alas for him
Who faints despite Thy pattern, King of Saints!
Alas alas for me the one that faints!

Lord, give us strength
To hold Thee fast until we hear Thy voice,
Which Thine own know who hearing it rejoice.

Lord, give us strength
To hold Thee fast until we see Thy Face,
Full fountain of all rapture and all grace.

But, when our strength
Shall be made darkness, and our bodies clay,
Hold Thou us fast and give us sleep till day.

"None other Lamb, none other Name"

None other Lamb, none other Name,
　None other Hope in heaven or earth or sea,
None other Hiding-place from guilt and shame,
　None beside Thee.

My faith burns low, my hope burns low,
　Only my heart's desire cries out in me
By the deep thunder of its want and woe,
　Cries out to Thee.

Lord, Thou art Life tho' I be dead,
　Love's Fire Thou art, however cold I be:
Nor heaven have I, nor place to lay my head,
　Nor home, but Thee.

Emily Dickinson (1830–1886)

"I never saw a moor"

I never saw a moor,
I never saw the sea;
Yet know I how the heather looks,
And what a wave must be.

I never spoke with God,
Nor visited in heaven;
Yet certain am I of the spot
As if the chart were given.

∿

Helen Hunt Jackson (1830–1885)

Doubt

They bade me cast the thing away,
They pointed to my hands all bleeding,
They listened not to all my pleading;
  The thing I meant I could not say:
  I knew that I should rue the day
  If once I cast that thing away.

I grasped it firm, and bore the pain;
The thorny husks I stripped and scattered;
If I could reach its heart, what mattered
  If other men saw not my gain,
  Or even if I should be slain?
  I knew the risks; I chose the pain.

Oh, had I cast that thing away,
I had not found what most I cherish,
A faith without which I should perish,
   The faith which, like a kernel, lay
   Hid in the husks which on that day
   My instinct would not throw away!

Gerard Manley Hopkins (1844–1889)

God's Grandeur

The world is charged with the grandeur of God.
   It will flame out, like shining from shook foil;
   It gathers to a greatness, like the ooze of oil
Crushed. Why do men then now not reck his rod?
Generations have trod, have trod, have trod;
   And all is seared with trade; bleared, smeared with toil;
   And wears man's smudge and shares man's smell: the soil
Is bare now, nor can foot feel, being shod.

And for all this, nature is never spent;
   There lives the dearest freshness deep down things;
And though the last lights off the black West went
   Oh, morning, at the brown brink eastward, springs—
Because the Holy Ghost over the bent
   World broods with warm breast and with ah! bright
     wings.

(Carrion Comfort)

Not, I'll not, carrion comfort, Despair, not feast on thee;
Not untwist—slack they may be—these last strands of man
In me ór, most weary, cry I *can no more*. I can;
Can something, hope, wish day come, not choose not to be.
But ah, but O thou terrible, why wouldst thou rude on me
Thy wring-world right foot rock? lay a lionlimb against me?
    scan
With darksome devouring eyes my bruisèd bones? and fan,
O in turns of tempest, me heaped there; me frantic to avoid
    thee and flee?

   Why? That my chaff might fly; my grain lie, sheer and
     clear.
Nay in all that toil, that coil, since (seems) I kissed the rod,
Hand rather, my heart lo! lapped strength, stole joy, would
    laugh, chéer.
Cheer whom though? the hero whose heaven-handling flung
    me, fóot tród
Me? or me that fought him? O which one? is it each one?
    That night, that year
Of now done darkness I wretch lay wrestling with (my God!)
    my God.

"Thou art indeed just, Lord, if I contend"

Thou art indeed just, Lord, if I contend
With thee; but, sir, so what I plead is just.

Why do sinners' ways prosper? and why must
Disappointment all I endeavour end?
 Wert thou my enemy, O thou my friend,
How wouldst thou worse, I wonder, than thou dost
Defeat, thwart me? Oh, the sots and thralls of lust
Do in spare hours more thrive than I that spend,
Sir, life upon thy cause. See, banks and brakes
Now, leavèd how thick! lacèd they are again
With fretty chervil, look, and fresh wind shakes
Them; birds build—but not I build; no, but strain,
Time's eunuch, and not breed one work that wakes.
Mine, O thou lord of life, send my roots rain.

∽

Robert Bridges (1844–1930)

"My eyes for beauty pine"

My eyes for beauty pine,
 My souls for Goddës grace:
No other care nor hope is mine;
 To heaven I turn my face.

One splendour thence is shed
 From all the stars above:
'Tis namèd when God's name is said,
 'Tis Love, 'tis heavenly Love.

And every gentle heart,
That burns with true desire,
Is lit from eyes that mirror part
Of that celestial fire.

Digby Mackworth Dolben (1848–1867)

Requests

I asked for Peace—
My sins arose,
And bound me close,
I could not find release.

I asked for Truth—
My doubts came in,
And with their din
They wearied all my youth.

I asked for Love—
My lovers failed,
And griefs assailed
Around, beneath, above.

I asked for Thee—
And Thou didst come
To take me home
Within Thy heart to be.

Flowers for the Altar

I

Tell us, tell us, holy shepherds,
    What at Bethlehem you saw.—
"Very God of Very God
    "Asleep amid the straw."

Tell us, tell us, all ye faithful,
    What this morning came to pass
At the awful elevation
    In the Canon of the Mass.—
"Very God of Very God,
    "By whom the worlds were made,
"In silence and in helplessness
    "Upon the altar laid."

Tell us, tell us, wondrous Jesu,
    What has drawn Thee from above
To the manger and the altar.—
    All the silence answers—Love.

II

Through the roaring streets of London
    Thou art passing, hidden Lord,
Uncreated, Consubstantial,
    In the seventh heaven adored.

As of old the ever-Virgin
    Through unconscious Bethlehem
Bore Thee, not in glad procession,
    Jewelled robe and diadem;
Not in pomp and not in power,
    Onward to Nativity,
Shrined but in the tabernacle
    Of her sweet Virginity.

Still Thou goest by in silence,
    Still the world cannot receive,
Still the poor and weak and weary
    Only, worship and believe.

✑

George Santayana (1863–1952)

"O world, thou choosest not the better part!"

O world, thou choosest not the better part!
It is not wisdom to be only wise,
And on the inward vision close the eyes,
But it is wisdom to believe the heart.
Columbus found a world, and had no chart,
Save one that faith deciphered in the skies;
To trust the soul's invincible surmise
Was all his science and his only art.

Our knowledge is a torch of smoky pine
That lights the pathway but one step ahead
Across a void of mystery and dread.
Bid, then, the tender light of faith to shine
By which alone the mortal heart is led
Unto the thinking of the thought divine.

∽

Gilbert K. Chesterton (1874–1936)

A Hymn

O God of earth and altar,
   Bow down and hear our cry,
Our earthly rules falter,
   Our people drift and die;
The walls of gold entomb us,
   The swords of scorn divide,
Take not thy thunder from us,
   But take away our pride.

From all that terror teaches,
   From lies of tongue and pen,
From all the easy speeches
   That comfort cruel men,
From sale and profanation
   Of honour and the sword,
From sleep and from damnation,
   Deliver us, good Lord!

Tie in a living tether
    The prince and priest and thrall,
Bind all our lives together,
    Smite us and save us all;
In ire and exultation
    Aflame with faith, and free,
Lift up a living nation,
    A single sword to thee.

Alphabetical List of Titles and First Lines

(Titles are given, in italics, only when distinct from the first lines.)

143